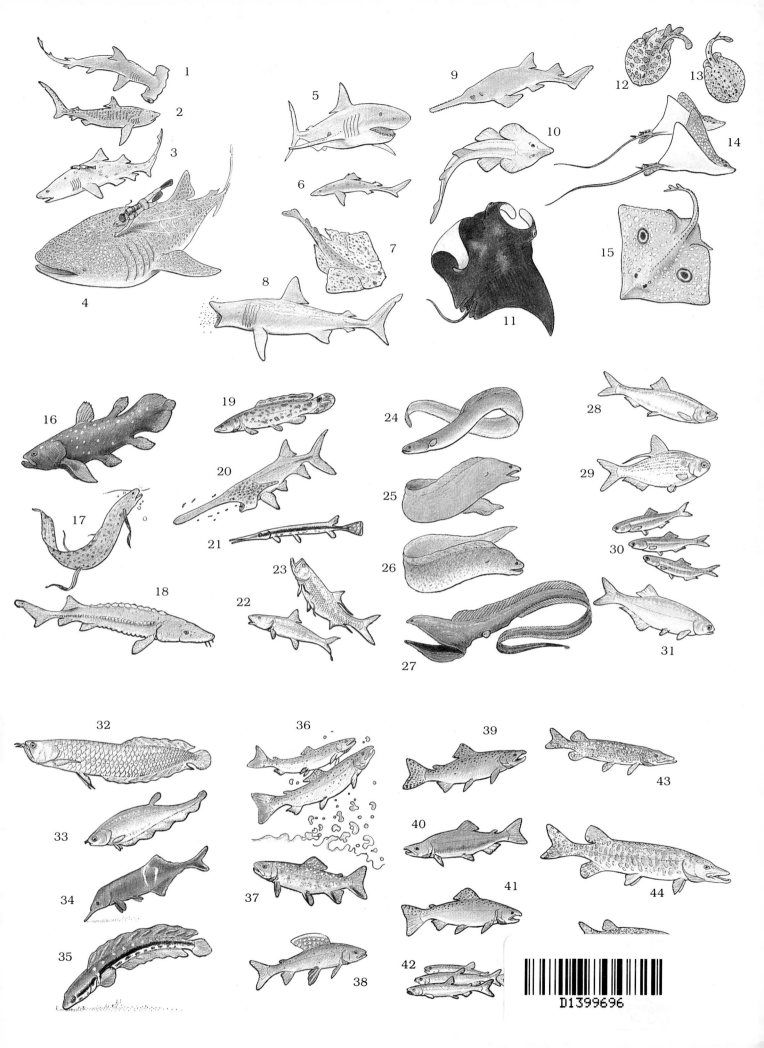

A Field Guide
to Fishes
Coloring Book

Sarah B. Landry

Illustrated by Sarah B. Landry

Roger Tory Peterson, Consulting Editor

*Sponsored by
the National Wildlife Federation,
the National Audubon Society,
and the Roger Tory Peterson Institute*

Houghton Mifflin Company   Boston

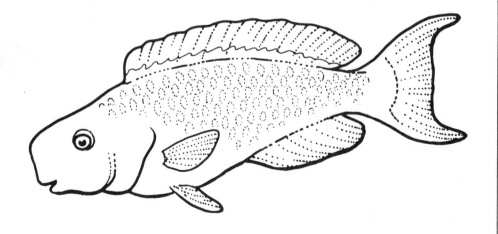

Printed in the United States of America

DPI 11 10 9 8 7 6 5 4 3

Introduction

Exploring the natural world is a visual activity; it trains the eye. Most budding naturalists soon acquire a copy of one or more of the Peterson Field Guides, such as the *Field Guide to Atlantic Coast Fishes* or *Pacific Coast Fishes*. These handy pocket-sized books offer shortcuts to identification, reducing things to basic shapes and patterns, with arrows pointing to the special field marks by which one species can be separated from another.

Although even a person who is colorblind can become skilled at identifying birds or mammals by their shapes and patterns, and flowers and trees by their leaves and other structures, for most of us color is the first clue. The Peterson Field Guide Coloring Books will sharpen your observations and condition your memory for the days you spend outdoors. By filling in the colors during evenings at home or on rainy days, you will be better informed about the animals and plants when you see them in life. Binoculars are a big help if you have a pair; a seven- or eight-power glass makes a bird or mammal seven or eight times as handsome, but it is not necessary for plants, insects, or fishes.

This coloring book will help your color perception and enable you to recognize the common fishes of North America. If you want to learn how to draw, you might try copying the basic line drawings so skillfully prepared by Sarah Landry. You could even try to sketch things in the field, if only roughly in pencil.

Exploring nature can be many things — an art, a science, a game, or a sport — but above all it is an absorbing activity that sharpens the senses, especially the eye and the ear. If you draw or paint, the sense of touch also comes into play; the images of the eye and the mind are transferred by hand to paper. In the process you become more aware of the natural world — the real world — and inevitably you become an environmentalist.

Most of you will find colored pencils best suited for coloring this book, but if you are handy with brushes and paints, you may prefer to fill in the outlines with watercolors. Crayons can also be used. But don't labor; have fun.

Roger Tory Peterson

About This Book

Fish Watching

Until quite recently, most people in North America thought that fishes were drab creatures. The feathers of a bird or the scales on the wings of a butterfly will keep their colors after the animal has died because the pigment in a feather or a wing scale (or in your own hair) is more or less unchangeable. But fishes are different.

Fish colors exist within a living cell. When a fish dies, the color factory closes down. Many of the colors the cell produced in life alter or fade. In earlier times most people saw fishes only in the market, in their kitchens, or on their dinner plates. These faded fishes were not colorful at all — or so it seemed. Only a privileged few knew differently.

In 1943 a revolution in fish watching occurred. People entered the water with the aid of a self-contained underwater breathing apparatus called SCUBA, and took their cameras with them. New kinds of pictures appeared in books, magazines, and films, revealing the fascinating colors and patterns of live fishes — some bold and bright, others so well camouflaged that they were nearly invisible.

Public interest in fishes grew. Modern pumps and filters made it easier to keep fishes alive in aquariums. The secret that fishermen, children along the shores of the South Pacific, and a few scientists and scientific artists had known all along — that fishes were just as beautiful as birds and butterflies — became known to the rest of us.

The bright tropical fishes were not the only ones that surprised us with their colors. The humblest northern minnow can shimmer with iridescent blues and greens, sparkle with flecks of orange, and glow with yellows — if only we can see it alive.

We hope this book will encourage you to look at fishes in a new way. By coloring the drawings in this book, you will not only learn something about fishes and how to identify them, but will also sharpen your powers of observation.

How to Use This Book

Coloring the Drawings.   Each fish in this book has a code number (in **boldface type** at the end of each description) which matches a colored drawing at the front or back of the book. You can refer to these models as you start to color, but don't worry about matching them exactly. Even in nature, the colors of fishes can vary. Have fun as you color the drawings. I hope you will enjoy recreating the natural colors of fishes as much as I do.

Guppy
(90)

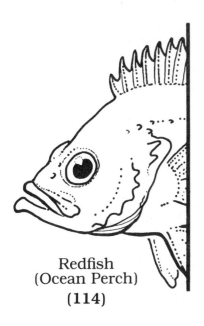

Redfish
(Ocean Perch)
(114)

Some general hints about coloring are listed below. If you want to know more about an individual fish, public aquariums, pet shops, field guides and other books and magazines can give you further information about fishes and the way they look.

- Many descriptions in this book contain words like "yellow-green" or "reddish black." *Enjoy experimenting.* Remember that fish themselves can vary.
- Colored pencils are probably the best way for you to color the pictures in this book. *Apply your colors lightly at first.* Start with pale, faint colors and gradually build up to stronger, darker colors.
- *Use white or cream or other pale-colored pencils to blend the colors beneath.* Then add more color on top of the blended colors. Try this technique on the little guppy in the margin.
- Notice that silver colored pencils don't automatically create a silvery effect. These metallic-colored pencils are useful, but they are too dark to be used alone. *Look at a piece of aluminum foil.* You will see that in some places it is the same kind of gray as a silver colored pencil, but in many other places it seems to be a pure, bright *white.* Furthermore, some silvers are warm and some are cool. All reflect other colors that are near them.
- *Eyes are more fun if you make them sparkle.* The sharp-eyed among you will notice that in life, a fish's eyes sparkle only if they are near a bright, focused light source. Still, it's fun to make them sparkle. It helps bring your drawing to life. Practice on the Redfish in the margin by leaving a white gleam in the dotted area near the center of its eye.
- *In nature many things are speckled.* You can imitate nature's color by stippling with your colored pencils. Using the pencil's point, firmly apply many little dots of color on top of the color underneath. By doing this you can create little clusters of pigment on paper, just as the fish's body has created little clusters of pigment in its skin.

Fishes Included. Most of the animals in this book are native North American fishes. Some live in fresh water; others are marine (ocean-dwelling). Some of them, like the fascinating fishes that live far offshore in the open ocean, are not animals you are going to see every day. In fact, you will be immensely lucky to see one of them in your lifetime. But it is nice to know they are out there. The geographic range of each fish is usually given in the description. Many of the more tropical Atlantic fishes are found throughout the Caribbean region as well as off our own coastline.

A small number of fishes in this book are "exotic" (non-native) fishes. Most of us are more likely to see exotic fishes in an aquarium or a picture than we are to see the little madtom catfish that lives in the pond across town. This is one reason exotic fishes have been included in this book.

Arrangement. Fishes in this book are arranged in large groups called orders . Members of these groups tend to share more physical traits with each other than they do with members of another group. It is handy to be able to group things together because they resemble one another. As scientists learn more about fishes, they sometimes shift an animal from one group to another.

About Fishes

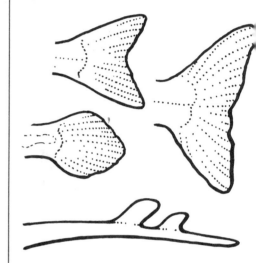

- Fishes are a class (very large group) of legless, aquatic animals. Like other vertebrates (animals with backbones), fishes have a skeleton supported by a backbone. Most-fishes have a bony skeleton but others, like sharks and rays and certain primitive fishes, have a skeleton made of cartilage.
- In place of legs, fishes have fins for locomotion. Some fishes have more fins than others, but all have a tail.
- Fishes have gills. A fish's gills take oxygen from the water the same way our lungs extract oxygen from the air. Fishes take both oxygen and nitrogen from their surroundings and give off waste carbon dioxide in return.
- Fishes have a two-chambered heart. A fish's heart pumps blood around its body more slowly than our more efficient heart pumps blood. This slower blood flow is one reason why fish are cold-blooded. A fish also converts food to energy more slowly. Because of this slower metabolic rate, a fish's body generates less heat, and its slow-moving blood has time to pick up the temperature of its surroundings. Like other warm-blooded animals, we are able to maintain our body temperature in spite of changes in our surroundings. Some fish are slightly warm-blooded, but most are cold-blooded.
- There are from 20,000 to 26,000 species of fishes in the world. In total numbers, there are more fishes on Earth than birds or mammals or reptiles or amphibians. These species of fish in turn are grouped by scientists into about 400 families worldwide. These families in turn are grouped into about 35 larger groups called orders, such as "Salmon and Their Kin" (known to scientists as Salmoniformes) or "Catfishes" (Siluriformes).
- Fishes come in a wide range of sizes and shapes. They can range in size from a 9-millimeter (5/16-inch) goby to an 18-meter (60-foot) Whale Shark (see p. 8).
- About 40% of fishes live in fresh water and about 60% live in salt water. Some fishes spend part of their lives in both.

- Most fishes have protective scales or bony plates that come in different sizes and shapes and arrangements. Other fishes have no scales at all but have thick skins and layers of mucus for protection.

Fishes have many of the same senses and organs found in other animals and people. You can pick out these familiar organs and features in the internal anatomy drawing below.

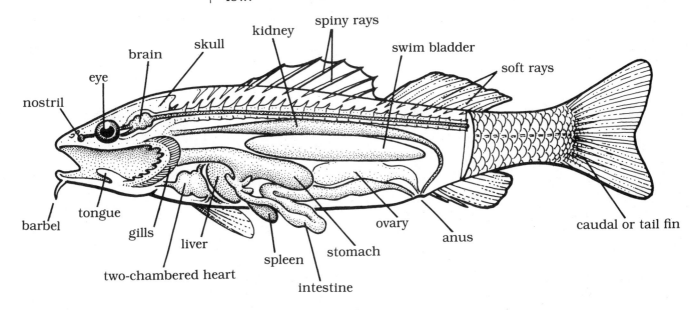

However, fishes also have some special organs and abilities that are unique.
- Some fishes have fleshy, whisker-like chin barbels or fleshy, sensitive areas on their skin. These can be used to probe the bottom for food or to feel changes in their environment.
- Other fishes have electrical organs on their bodies. Some, like the mormyrids (p. 17), use these organs to scan their murky habitats, much the way radar scans for objects hidden in the night. Other fishes pack a stronger electrical charge and use it to protect themselves or to stun their prey.
- All fishes have either a lateral line (see drawing at left) or isolated sensory pores that tell the fish when the water around it is being disturbed.
- A fish's swim bladder is one of its most unique and vital organs. This long, oxygen-and nitrogen-filled organ is linked with the fish's bloodstream by means of tiny capillaries. Fish use this marvelous balloon to adjust their buoyancy, so that they don't have to work to maintain their floating level. Sharks and rays have no swim bladders. Body oils help some sharks float, but most overcome their tendency to sink by swimming actively.

A typical spiny-rayed fish is shown at left.

Typical Spiny-rayed Fish

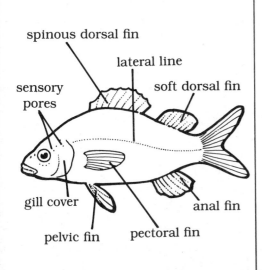

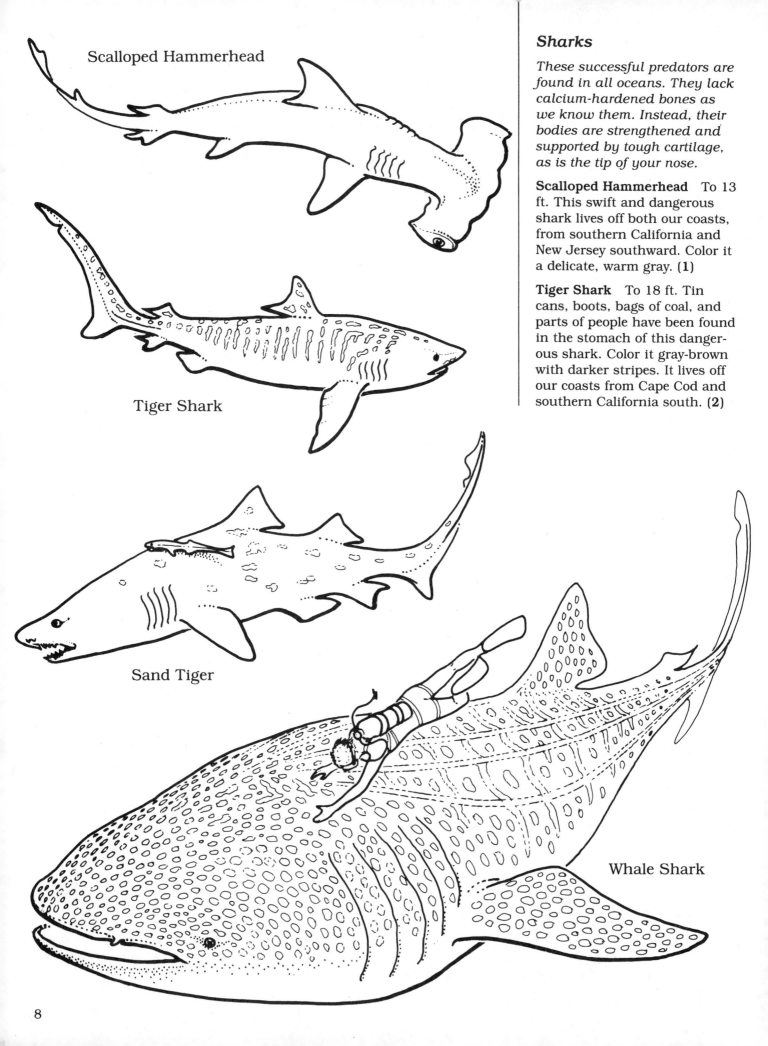

Scalloped Hammerhead

Tiger Shark

Sand Tiger

Whale Shark

Sharks

These successful predators are found in all oceans. They lack calcium-hardened bones as we know them. Instead, their bodies are strengthened and supported by tough cartilage, as is the tip of your nose.

Scalloped Hammerhead   To 13 ft. This swift and dangerous shark lives off both our coasts, from southern California and New Jersey southward. Color it a delicate, warm gray. (**1**)

Tiger Shark   To 18 ft. Tin cans, boots, bags of coal, and parts of people have been found in the stomach of this dangerous shark. Color it gray-brown with darker stripes. It lives off our coasts from Cape Cod and southern California south. (**2**)

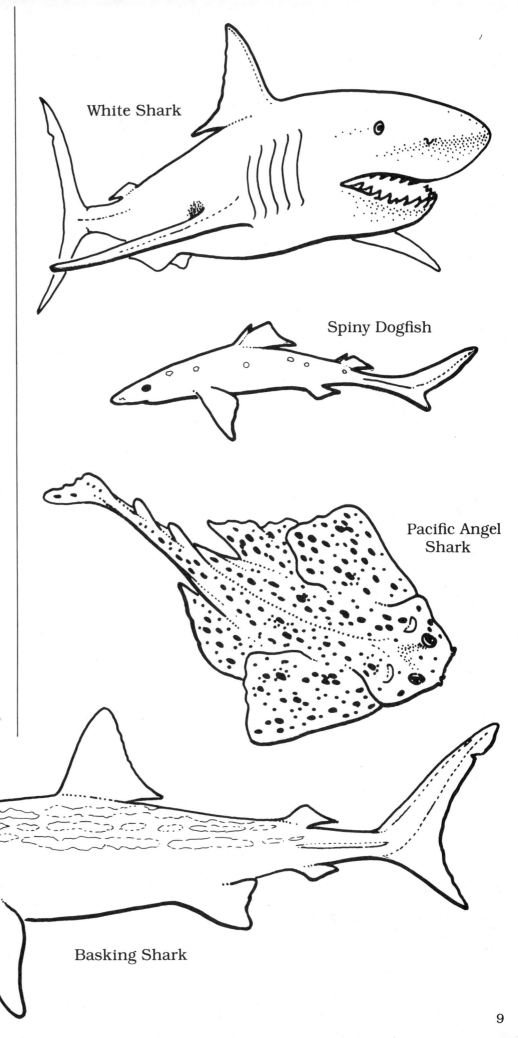

Sand Tiger To 10½ ft. This sluggish but large shark looks as if it needs to visit an orthodontist. It is found off the Atlantic Coast from Maine southward. **(3)**

Whale Shark To 60 ft. This huge and peaceful shark is found worldwide in warmish waters. It is the world's largest fish. It cruises with its mouth open, filtering its food from the ocean's plankton soup. Color it bluish or brownish gray with soft white spots. **(4)**

White Shark To 21 ft. This aggressive shark feeds on large and small animals alike — including people. Turnabout is fair play: in some parts or the world, people eat White Sharks. This shark is found off both our coasts from Nova Scotia and Alaska south. **(5)**

Spiny Dogfish To 5 ft. Found worldwide and off both our coasts in cool waters, this small shark is gray with dime-sized white spots. **(6)**

Pacific Angel Shark To 5 ft. This bottom-loving shark lives in shallow waters from Washington south. Color it beige, mottled with brown and speckled with black. **(7)**

Basking Shark To 45 ft. This huge, placid shark is found worldwide in cool waters. Like the Whale Shark, it filters plankton from the water. Color it gray with paler stripes. **(8)**

White Shark

Spiny Dogfish

Pacific Angel Shark

Basking Shark

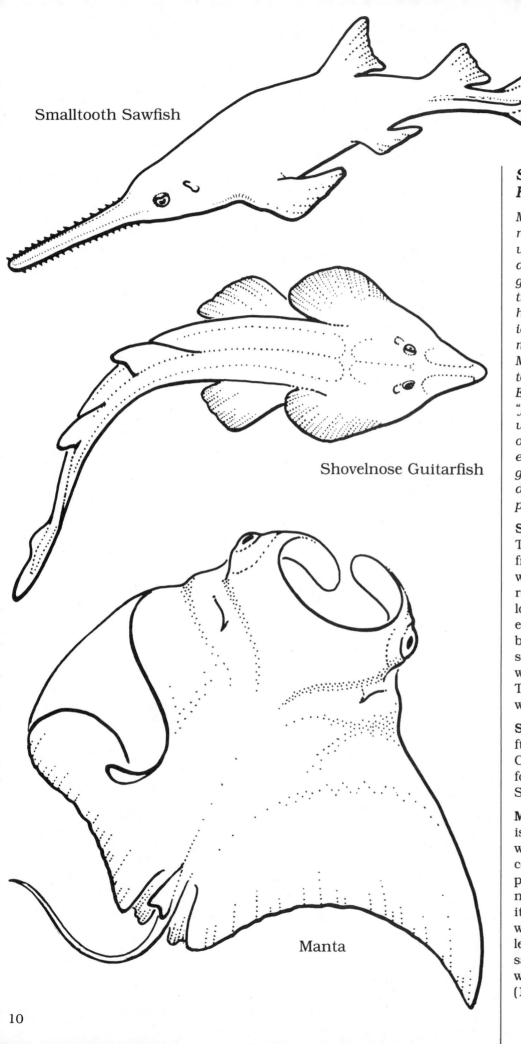

Smalltooth Sawfish

Shovelnose Guitarfish

Manta

Skates, Rays, and Their Kin

Most of this group of cartilaginous fishes are flat-bodied, with large pectoral fins joined directly to their heads. Their gill slits are underneath and their spiracles (water-intake holes) are on top of their bodies. Most of these fishes are marine (ocean-dwelling). Many live on or near the bottom; others, like the splendid Eagle and Manta rays, can "fly" gracefully through the water. Some rays have venomous spines on their tails. Others have special electric organs, which they use for defense and to shock their prey.

Smalltooth Sawfish To 18 ft. This Atlantic sawfish is found from the Chesapeake south and worldwide in warm seas. It roots through sand or mud, looking for small creatures to eat. Sometimes it slashes its bony, toothed nose through schools of fish, disabling some, which it then eats at its leisure. This fish is gray above and white below. **(9)**

Shovelnose Guitarfish To 5½ ft. This sand-colored Pacific Coast guitarfish is usually found buried in the mud from San Francisco southward. **(10)**

Manta To 22 ft. This large ray is found in warm water worldwide. It lives off both our coasts. A Manta uses the long projections on its head to funnel plankton and shrimp into its mouth. It is black-backed with a white belly. When it leaps from the water it somersaults or belly-flops back in with a tremendous *thwack.* **(11)**

Lesser Electric Ray To 18 in. If you step on this pretty little ray, it will give you a 37-volt shock. But consider yourself lucky — some of its relatives carry a dangerous 220-volt charge. This ray lives in sandy surf zones along the Atlantic Coast from North Carolina south through the Gulf of Mexico. Color it sandy brown with darker blotches that are ringed with black spots. **(12)**

Yellow Stingray To 14 in. If you step on *this* ray, it will jab you with a painfully venomous barb on its tail. In shallow waters where it lives, off Florida and into the Caribbean, people shuffle, rather than walk, to avoid stepping on it. It is beige with yellow spots and many tiny, wormlike speckles. **(13)**

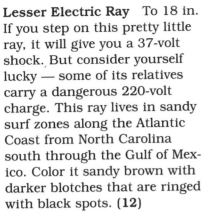

Yellow Stingray

Lesser Electric Ray

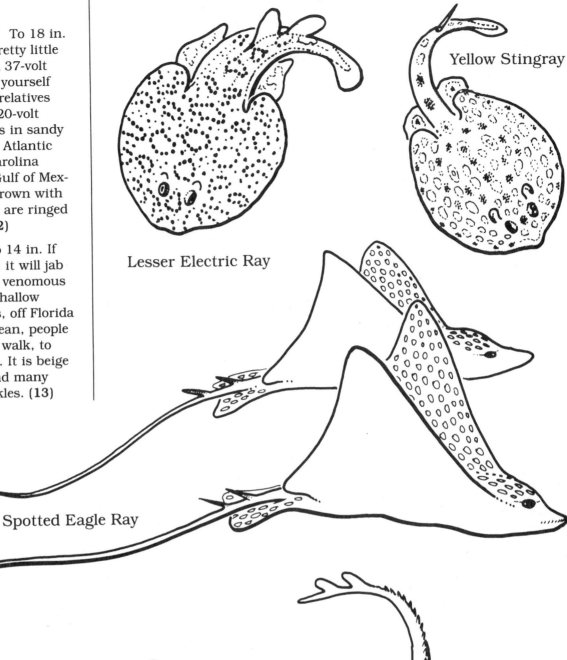

Spotted Eagle Ray

Big Skate

Spotted Eagle Ray To 9 ft. This elegant large ray is normally solitary but migrates in large groups. It lives worldwide in warmish waters. Unlike most rays, it has a large and distinct head. It has two barbs on its tail. Color this ray olive or chestnut brown with bluish white spots. **(14)**

Big Skate To 8 ft. This Pacific skate is one of North America's largest. It is found widely from the Bering Sea south. Color it reddish or greenish beige with white spots and huge eyespots on its pectoral fins. **(15)**

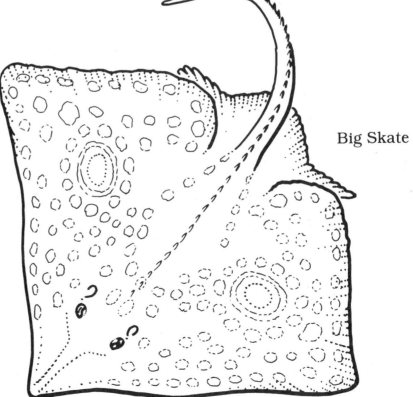

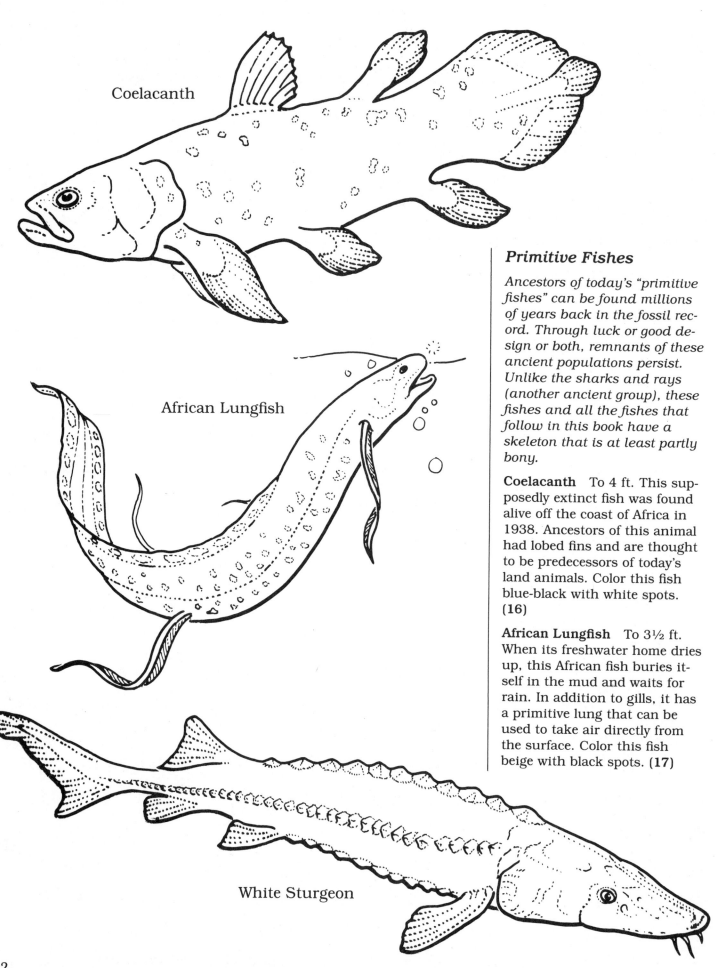

Coelacanth

African Lungfish

White Sturgeon

Primitive Fishes

Ancestors of today's "primitive fishes" can be found millions of years back in the fossil record. Through luck or good design or both, remnants of these ancient populations persist. Unlike the sharks and rays (another ancient group), these fishes and all the fishes that follow in this book have a skeleton that is at least partly bony.

Coelacanth To 4 ft. This supposedly extinct fish was found alive off the coast of Africa in 1938. Ancestors of this animal had lobed fins and are thought to be predecessors of today's land animals. Color this fish blue-black with white spots. **(16)**

African Lungfish To 3½ ft. When its freshwater home dries up, this African fish buries itself in the mud and waits for rain. In addition to gills, it has a primitive lung that can be used to take air directly from the surface. Color this fish beige with black spots. **(17)**

White Sturgeon To 12½ ft. We pay $60 an ounce for this sturgeon's eggs and call them caviar. Huge sturgeons used to be found in North America, but were overfished. Today, the White Sturgeons found near river mouths on the Pacific Northwest coast are a more modest size. Color yours greenish gray with a white belly. **(18)**

Bowfin To 3 ft. This greenish brown-mottled fish lives in still waters in the Mississippi region. Breeding males have an orange border around the black spot on the tail. **(19)**

Paddlefish To 7 ft. This preposterous-looking brown fish lives largely on plankton in the Missisippi River region. **(20)**

Longnose Gar To 6 ft. Gars lie as motionless as logs and wait for prey (small fish). This gar is olive-brown above and white below, with a dark, blotched line from nose to tail. It lives in quiet fresh water in the central and southern states. **(21)**

Bonefish To 3 ft. This sport fish is common in marine shallows off southern Florida. It is silver with a faintly blue-green back and delicate dusky stripes on the sides. **(22)**

Tarpon To 8 ft. Found in shallow waters around Florida and the Gulf of Mexico and occasionally farther north, this famous sport fish leaps repeatedly from the water if hooked. It is silver. Study aluminum foil for inspiration and add a few reflected pinks and greens for beauty and fun. **(23)**

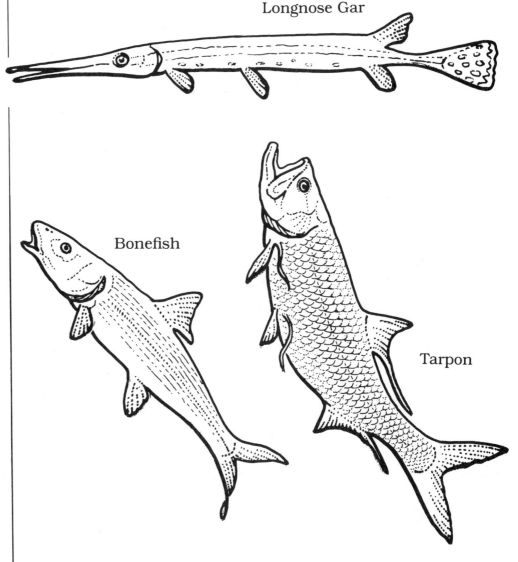

Bowfin

male

Paddlefish

Longnose Gar

Bonefish

Tarpon

13

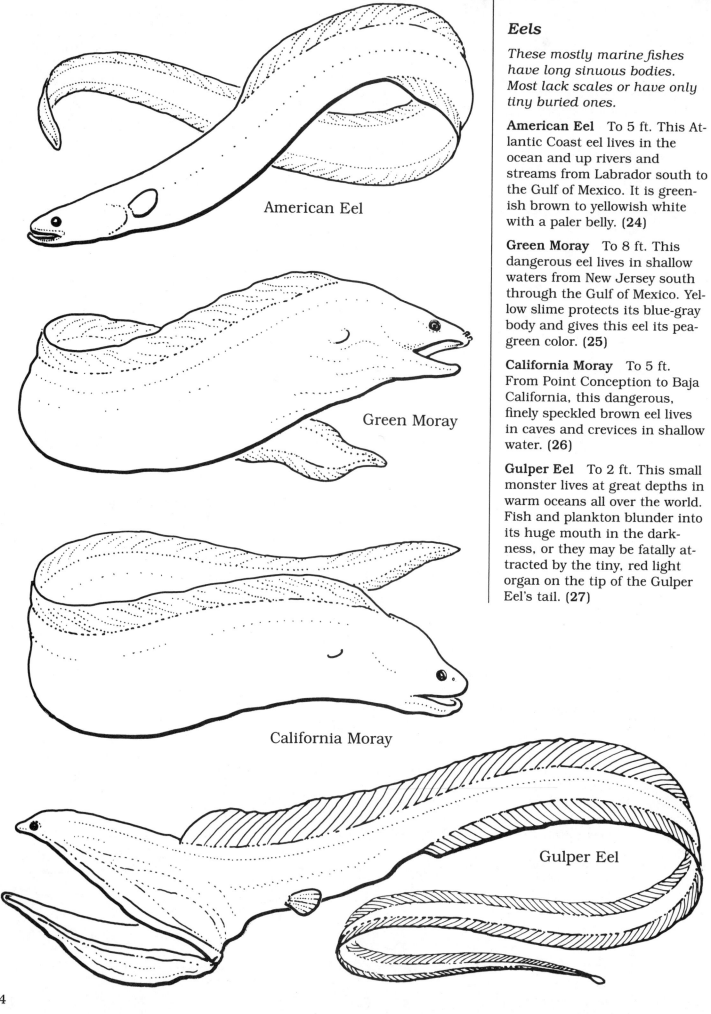

American Eel

Green Moray

California Moray

Gulper Eel

Eels

These mostly marine fishes have long sinuous bodies. Most lack scales or have only tiny buried ones.

American Eel   To 5 ft. This Atlantic Coast eel lives in the ocean and up rivers and streams from Labrador south to the Gulf of Mexico. It is greenish brown to yellowish white with a paler belly. **(24)**

Green Moray   To 8 ft. This dangerous eel lives in shallow waters from New Jersey south through the Gulf of Mexico. Yellow slime protects its blue-gray body and gives this eel its pea-green color. **(25)**

California Moray   To 5 ft. From Point Conception to Baja California, this dangerous, finely speckled brown eel lives in caves and crevices in shallow water. **(26)**

Gulper Eel   To 2 ft. This small monster lives at great depths in warm oceans all over the world. Fish and plankton blunder into its huge mouth in the darkness, or they may be fatally attracted by the tiny, red light organ on the tip of the Gulper Eel's tail. **(27)**

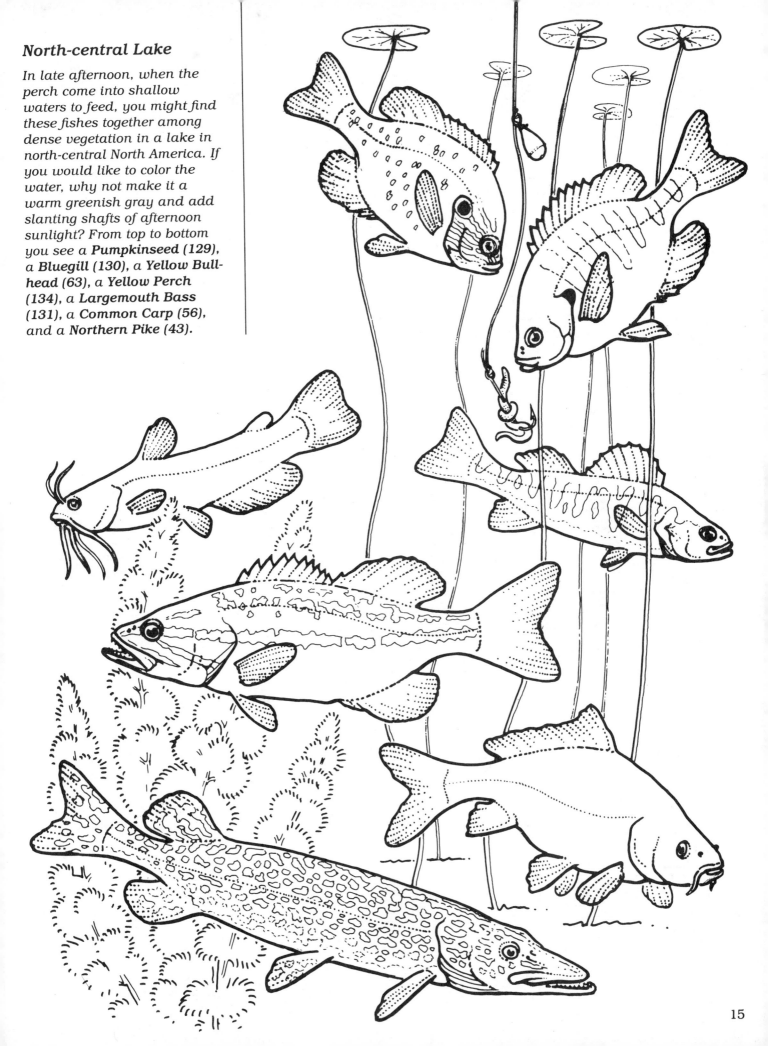

North-central Lake

In late afternoon, when the perch come into shallow waters to feed, you might find these fishes together among dense vegetation in a lake in north-central North America. If you would like to color the water, why not make it a warm greenish gray and add slanting shafts of afternoon sunlight? From top to bottom you see a **Pumpkinseed (129)**, a **Bluegill (130)**, a **Yellow Bullhead (63)**, a **Yellow Perch (134)**, a **Largemouth Bass (131)**, a **Common Carp (56)**, and a **Northern Pike (43)**.

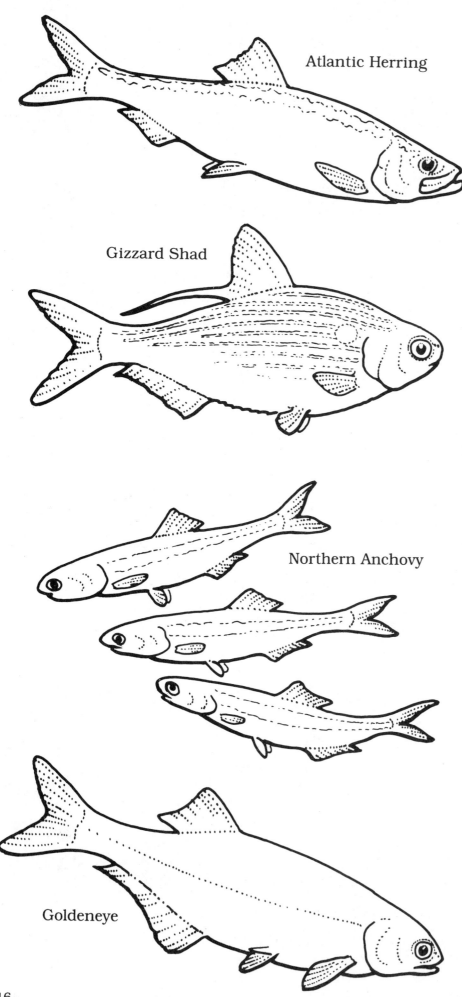

Atlantic Herring

Gizzard Shad

Northern Anchovy

Goldeneye

Herrings and Their Kin

Some members of this large group of mostly marine fishes live in immense schools. They are a very important food resource for fish and human predators alike.

Atlantic Herring To 16 in. Smoked, canned, used for fish meal and oil, this famous Atlantic fish has made the fortunes of families and influenced the course of European history. It is silvery with a bluish back and is found along our coast from Labrador south to Cape Hatteras. **(28)**

Gizzard Shad To 16 in. This herring has a blue-gray back and silvery sides. It lives in the southeastern and central states. It is primarily a freshwater fish but strays occasionally into salt water. **(29)**

Northern Anchovy To 9 in. The elite among us know the anchovy from the tops of pizzas. In life, this fish lives in huge shoals of its kin along the coast from British Columbia south to Baja California. Color it gun-metal blue to green, with a silvery stripe along its sides. **(30)**

Arawanas and Their Kin

Most members of this big-scaled, bony-headed group are freshwater tropical fishes.

Goldeneye To 20 in. This blue and silver fish is a mooneye, a northern relative in the arawana group. It lives in fresh water throughout large parts of Canada and the central United States. **(31)**

Arawana To 3½ ft. This stately and haughty-looking fish lives in lakes and quiet rivers in South America. Color it silver with touches of reflected pinks and yellows. Each large scale is edged with pink. **(32)**

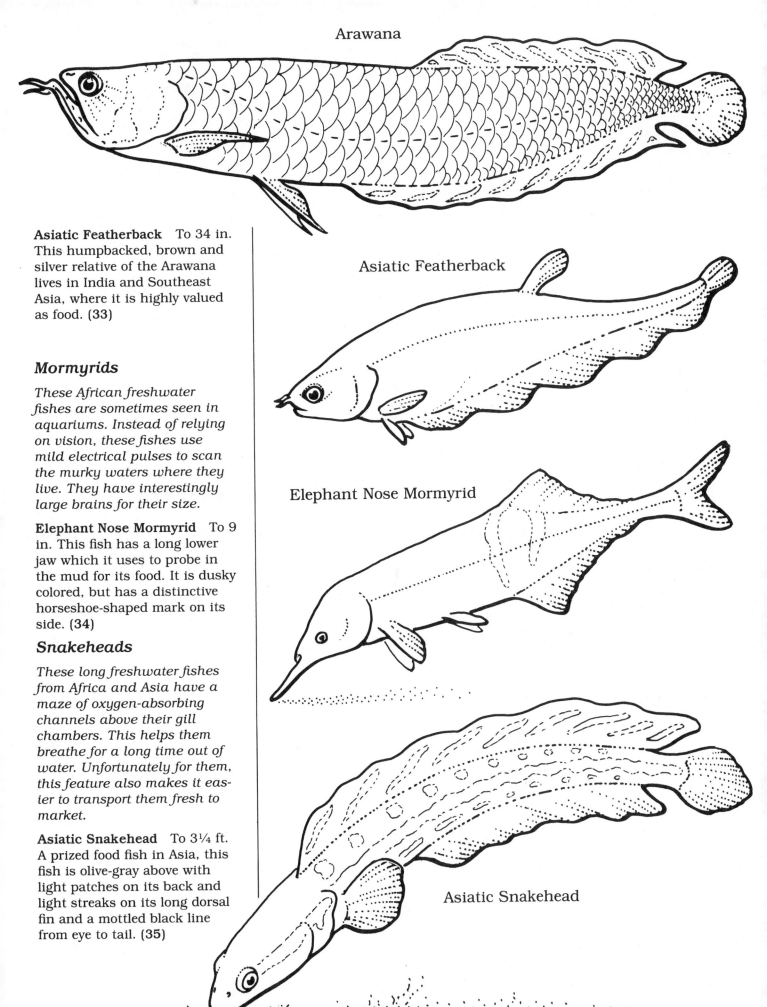

Arawana

Asiatic Featherback To 34 in. This humpbacked, brown and silver relative of the Arawana lives in India and Southeast Asia, where it is highly valued as food. **(33)**

Mormyrids

These African freshwater fishes are sometimes seen in aquariums. Instead of relying on vision, these fishes use mild electrical pulses to scan the murky waters where they live. They have interestingly large brains for their size.

Elephant Nose Mormyrid To 9 in. This fish has a long lower jaw which it uses to probe in the mud for its food. It is dusky colored, but has a distinctive horseshoe-shaped mark on its side. **(34)**

Snakeheads

These long freshwater fishes from Africa and Asia have a maze of oxygen-absorbing channels above their gill chambers. This helps them breathe for a long time out of water. Unfortunately for them, this feature also makes it easier to transport them fresh to market.

Asiatic Snakehead To 3¼ ft. A prized food fish in Asia, this fish is olive-gray above with light patches on its back and light streaks on its long dorsal fin and a mottled black line from eye to tail. **(35)**

Asiatic Featherback

Elephant Nose Mormyrid

Asiatic Snakehead

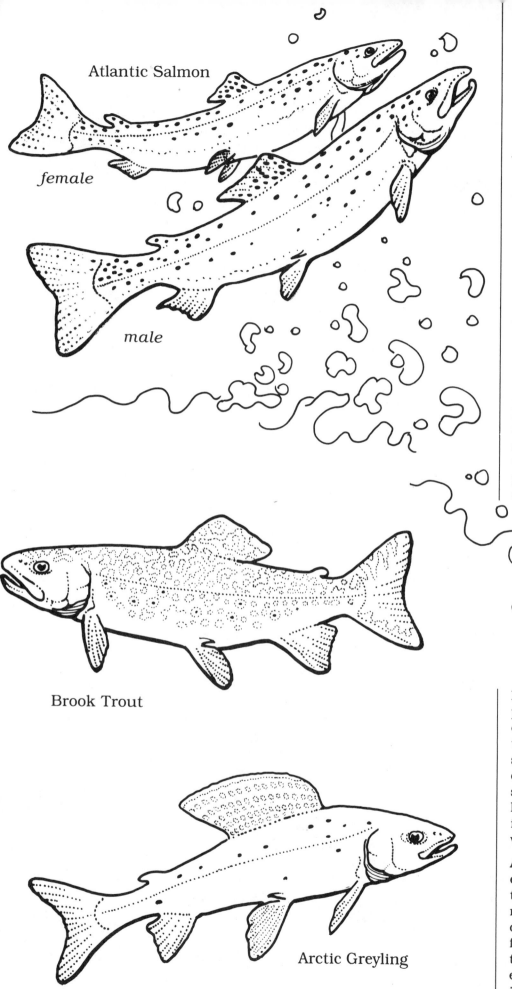

Atlantic Salmon

female

male

Brook Trout

Arctic Greyling

Salmon and Their Kin

Many of the fish in this group are commercially valuable or are good sport fish — or both. Most have no hard spines in their fins and have a small, fatty fin called an adipose fin between the dorsal fin and the tail. Members of this group live in fresh as well as salt water. Some, like the salmon, live parts of their lives in each. Deepwater marine forms of these fishes look very unlike their more familiar relatives and come as quite a surprise.

Atlantic Salmon To 4½ ft. As we win the battle against river pollution and build fishways around our dams, these great fish are slowly returning to East Coast rivers from Greenland south to Maine. Atlantic Salmon are brownish silver above with silver sides and dark spots. Males have reddish patches along their sides in spawning season. **(36)**

Brook Trout To 21 in. This pretty trout can be found from eastern North America through the Great Lakes region and southward into Georgia, in clear, cool streams. The red spots on its sides have blue halos and the leading edges of its reddish lower fins are bright white. **(37)**

Arctic Greyling To 30 in. In earlier times this big arctic trout was an important food for northern Indians and their dogs. It is found northward from the Great Lakes region. Its tall dorsal fin is spotted and edged with white and its body is a soft purple-gray. **(38)**

Chinook Salmon To 4 ft. 10 in. This famous Pacific salmon has many names: Chinook, King, Spring, and Tyee. It is the most highly prized Pacific Coast game fish. It is found from the Bering Sea to central California. Even at sea, where all salmon are blue-gray and silver, you can tell this fish by its black gums. Color this river-spawning male a dusky bronze above with a pinkish belly. **(39)**

Sockeye Salmon To 33 in. This commercially valuable salmon has no spots at all. It is found in the same area as the Chinook. The male's breeding color is an unmistakable pinky red with a greenish head. **(40)**

Coho Salmon To 3 ft. 3 in. This Pacific salmon has the same range as the other two great salmon. It can be distinguished from the Chinook by its white or grayish gums. The male's river-spawning color is a dusky bronze with red sides. **(41)**

Rainbow Smelt To 13 in. Like many of its trout and salmon cousins, this little fish spends its life in the ocean but spawns in fresh water. There are smelts on both our coasts. This one is found in the Atlantic from Labrador south to Virginia. It is said that these tasty little fish are so oily that a dried one will burn like a candle. One of the old names for this smelt is "Candlefish," so perhaps this is true. The Rainbow Smelt is bottle-green with a silver band from nose to tail. Let your silver band reflect other colors to make the "rainbow." **(42)**

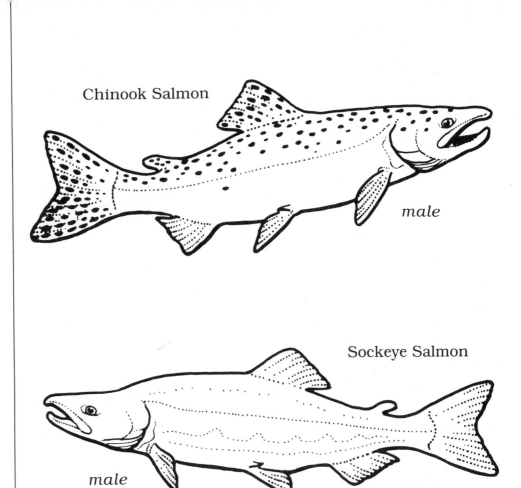

Chinook Salmon

male

Sockeye Salmon

male

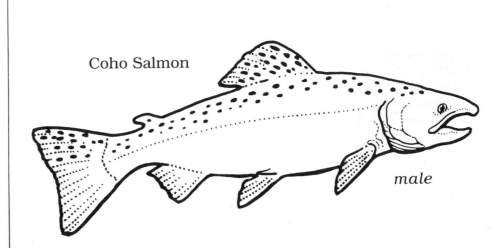

Coho Salmon

male

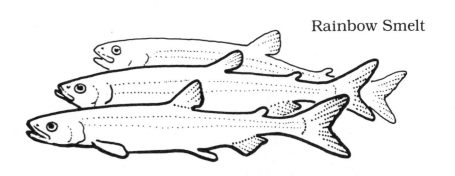

Rainbow Smelt

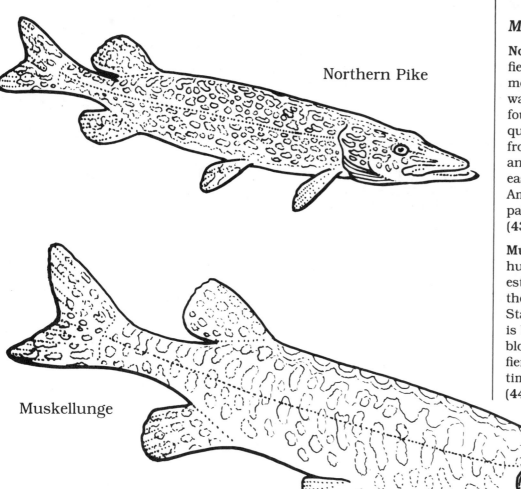

Northern Pike

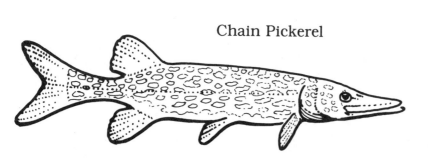

Muskellunge

Chain Pickerel

Central Mudminnow

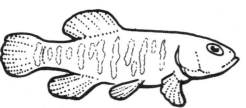

Northern Pike To 4 ft. This fierce, predatory pike is the most widely distributed freshwater fish in the world. It is found lurking in lakes and quiet parts of large streams from Alaska across to Labrador and down into large sections of eastern and central North America. It is greenish with pale spots and a white belly. (43)

Muskellunge To 6 ft. This huge freshwater fish is the largest in the pike family. It lives in the central and eastern United States and southern Canada. It is bronze-green with dusky blotches on its sides. It is as fierce as a barracuda and sometimes feeds on adult ducks. (44)

Chain Pickerel To 31 in. This greenish bronze little pike is found from Nova Scotia south to Florida and west into the Mississippi region in clean, quiet, weedy waters. It is often caught by ice fishermen in winter. Its body is spotted like that of a Northern Pike, but unlike the Northern Pike, the Pickerel has gill covers that are fully scaled. (In the Northern Pike only the upper third of each gill cover is scaled.) (45)

Central Mudminnow To 5 in. This small, stout and hardy carnivore is a survival specialist. It can stand low levels of oxygen and low temperatures. It lives in stagnant, silty pools in north-central states and well up into Canada. It is olive-brown with faint orange flecks in its fins and a dark bar at the base of its tail. (46)

Some Deepsea Fishes with Light Organs

By mixing chemicals together as in a light-stick, or by letting bacteria do it for them, many deepsea fishes have evolved light-producing organs. These organs are called photophores. These fishes use their lights to attract prey and also to find one another. In the world's oceans, a mile or more beneath the surface, in inky darkness and under great pressure, these animals conduct their lives. They are like creatures from another planet.

Deepsea Bristlemouth To 14 in. Millions of these small brownish fish with rows of tiny lights on their bodies live in the ocean's depths. **(47)**

Hatchetfish To 3 in. This cleaver-shaped, silvery little fish has large yellowish light organs on its body. **(48)**

Deepsea Viperfish To 5 in. This scaled viperfish has oversized fangs and a longish body. Why not color this one a purplish black with greenish light organs? **(49)**

Loosejawed Dragonfish To 10 in. These brownish black creatures have red or green light organs, including a large one behind their eyes. They often have extremely long chin barbels. This fish has no "floor" to its mouth at all. **(50)**

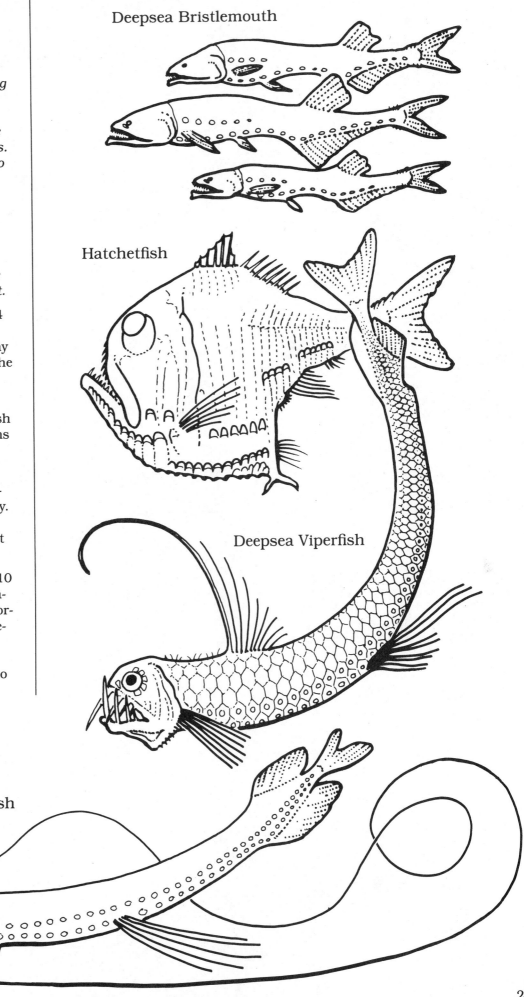

Deepsea Bristlemouth

Hatchetfish

Deepsea Viperfish

Loosejawed Dragonfish

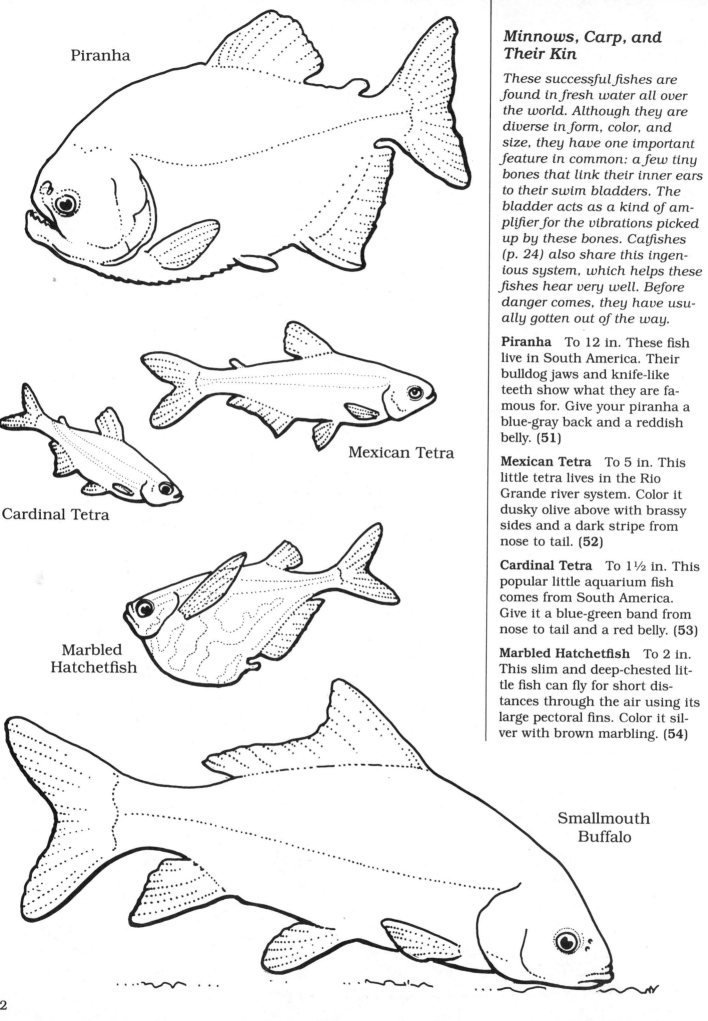

Piranha

Mexican Tetra

Cardinal Tetra

Marbled Hatchetfish

Smallmouth Buffalo

Minnows, Carp, and Their Kin

These successful fishes are found in fresh water all over the world. Although they are diverse in form, color, and size, they have one important feature in common: a few tiny bones that link their inner ears to their swim bladders. The bladder acts as a kind of amplifier for the vibrations picked up by these bones. Catfishes (p. 24) also share this ingenious system, which helps these fishes hear very well. Before danger comes, they have usually gotten out of the way.

Piranha To 12 in. These fish live in South America. Their bulldog jaws and knife-like teeth show what they are famous for. Give your piranha a blue-gray back and a reddish belly. (51)

Mexican Tetra To 5 in. This little tetra lives in the Rio Grande river system. Color it dusky olive above with brassy sides and a dark stripe from nose to tail. (52)

Cardinal Tetra To 1½ in. This popular little aquarium fish comes from South America. Give it a blue-green band from nose to tail and a red belly. (53)

Marbled Hatchetfish To 2 in. This slim and deep-chested little fish can fly for short distances through the air using its large pectoral fins. Color it silver with brown marbling. (54)

Smallmouth Buffalo   To 3 ft. Its large size and humped back give this fish its name. This blue-gray and bronze fish lives in deep channels in rivers throughout our central states. **(55)**

Common Carp   To 30 in. Introduced into this country 100 years ago, this adaptable fish is now found almost everywhere. Give yours an olive-gray back and a yellowish belly. **(56)**

Goldfish   To 6 in. Don't let your pet goldfish go. It can survive almost anywhere in fresh water and will eat the eggs of other fishes. Color the wild goldfish a dusky bronze and the pet goldfish orange. **(57)**

Sumatra Barb   To 2½ in. This pretty barb is a good beginner's aquarium fish. Give it black bars and red fins. **(58)**

Golden Shiner   To 12 in. This is North America's most common baitfish. It has a golden olive back and silver sides and can live in clear lakes and streams almost anywhere east of the Rockies. **(50)**

Southern Redbelly Dace   To 3 in. This pretty minnow is found in cool, clean streams in the central Mississippi River area. It has a golden-olive back with dark spots and a white stripe bordered with black lines. Males have a bright red belly in breeding season. **(60)**

White Sucker   To 2 ft. Widespread in central North America, this fish can be found vacuuming its food from the bottom of cool streams and lakes. It has a dusky-colored back and brassy sides. **(61)**

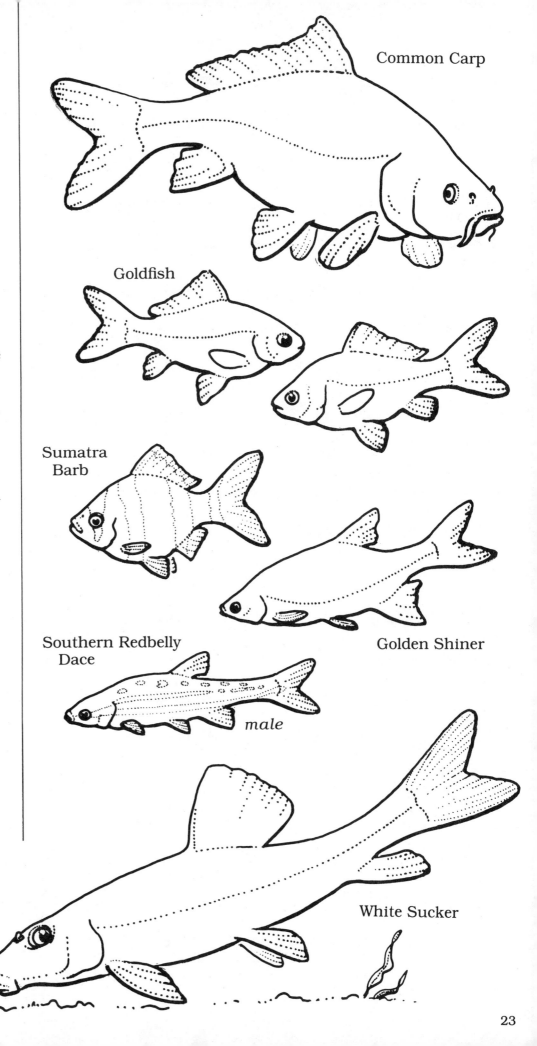

Common Carp

Goldfish

Sumatra Barb

Golden Shiner

Southern Redbelly Dace

male

White Sucker

23

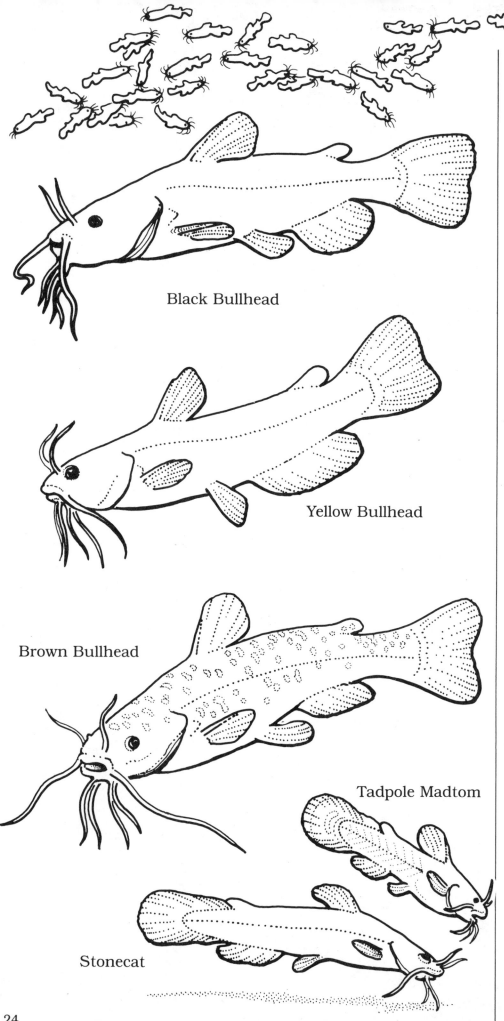

Black Bullhead

Yellow Bullhead

Brown Bullhead

Tadpole Madtom

Stonecat

Catfishes

This large group of mostly freshwater fishes is found all over the world. Most catfishes feed on the bottom, using their whisker-like barbels to probe for food. Like the salmon (p. 18), catfishes have a second little fin on their backs that is fleshy and not reinforced by rays or spines. Many catfishes — including our own innocent-looking madtoms — have venomous pectoral spines. Handle with care!

Black Bullhead To 17 in. Male bullheads are good fathers. They guard the eggs and then the young until they are quite large. This bullhead can be found in quiet waters over muddy bottoms in central North America. Color yours olive-black with a yellowish belly. His babies are black. **(62)**

Yellow Bullhead To 18 in. This bullhead is found in quiet waters and slow streams in central and eastern North America. It is olive-brown with a yellowish belly. Its chin barbels are white. **(63)**

Brown Bullhead To 19 in. This is the only bullhead with brown mottles on its sides and very long jaw barbels. It lives in clear deep water from Nova Scotia south and west through central North America. **(64)**

Tadpole Madtom To 4½ in. If you get poked by the pectoral spine of this wiggly little madtom, the wound will hurt for a long time. Madtoms can be found widely in all but the mountainous areas of eastern and central states. They are olive-gray. **(65)**

Stonecat To 12 in. This slate gray to olive-green cousin of the madtom can be found over stony bottoms in lakes and streams from the St. Lawrence south through central and western North America. Stonecats have white chins and venomous pectoral spines. **(66)**

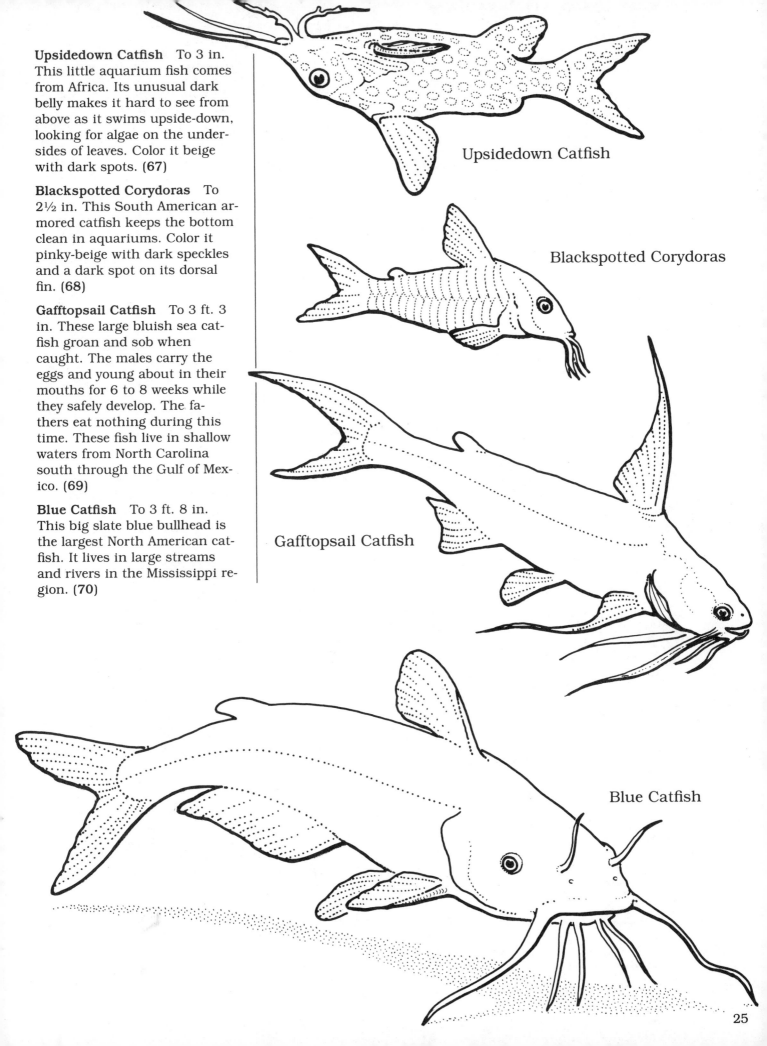

Upsidedown Catfish   To 3 in. This little aquarium fish comes from Africa. Its unusual dark belly makes it hard to see from above as it swims upside-down, looking for algae on the undersides of leaves. Color it beige with dark spots. **(67)**

Blackspotted Corydoras   To 2½ in. This South American armored catfish keeps the bottom clean in aquariums. Color it pinky-beige with dark speckles and a dark spot on its dorsal fin. **(68)**

Gafftopsail Catfish   To 3 ft. 3 in. These large bluish sea catfish groan and sob when caught. The males carry the eggs and young about in their mouths for 6 to 8 weeks while they safely develop. The fathers eat nothing during this time. These fish live in shallow waters from North Carolina south through the Gulf of Mexico. **(69)**

Blue Catfish   To 3 ft. 8 in. This big slate blue bullhead is the largest North American catfish. It lives in large streams and rivers in the Mississippi region. **(70)**

Upsidedown Catfish

Blackspotted Corydoras

Gafftopsail Catfish

Blue Catfish

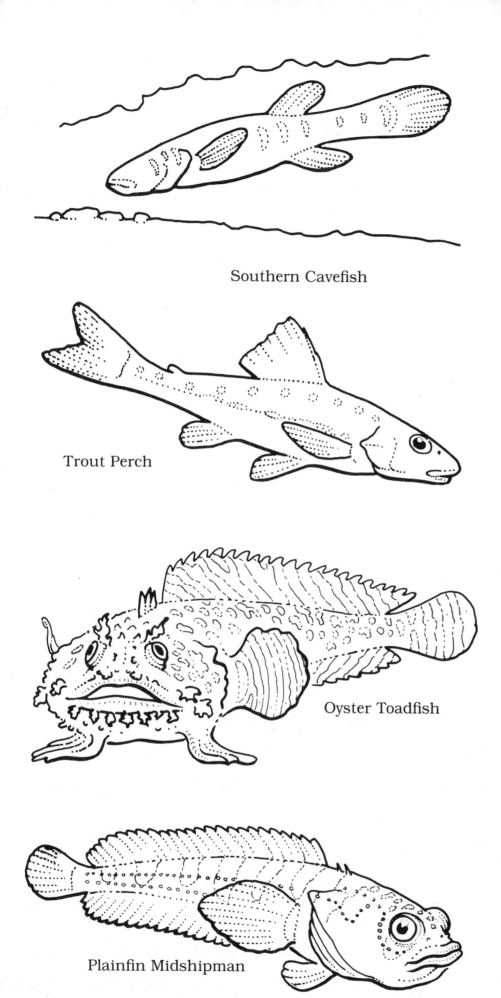

Southern Cavefish

Trout Perch

Oyster Toadfish

Plainfin Midshipman

Cavefishes, Trout Perches, and Their Kin

The smallish freshwater fishes in this group have weak spines in their dorsal fins. This and other features make them resemble the perch-like fishes you will find toward the end of this book.

Southern Cavefish To 3 in. Color this eyeless fish a very pale flesh tone. It lives in limestone caves in the Mississippi region of the south-central states. Sensitive extensions of its skin help this fish feel its way in the dark. (71)

Trout Perch To 6 in. This fish is found in lakes and streams from the Great Lakes region northward. It is a yellowish color with rows of dusky spots on its back. (72)

Toadfishes

These grumpy-looking, well-camouflaged marine fishes live on the bottom. Some can make quite loud noises, using their swim bladders as a bellows.

Oyster Toadfish To 15 in. This Atlantic toadfish lurks in the shallows from Cape Cod to Florida. It can bite hard with its sharp teeth. Color this one black and brown. (73)

Plainfin Midshipman To 15 in. Hundreds of these male toadfish can make quite an irritating and loud hum while trying to attract a mate, as some houseboat owners on the Pacific Coast have discovered. These bronzy-purple fish have large light organs under their chins. Why not show your fish casting a greenish glow on the bottom? These interesting fish live in shallow waters from Alaska to Baja California. (74)

Anglerfishes

This interesting group contains many marine fishes which have a modified dorsal fin that serves as a fishing pole. When a meal gets close, an anglerfish sucks it in with a fast and powerful gulp.

Sargassumfish To 6 in. This Atlantic fish lives amid clumps of sargassum weed far at sea from New England south through the Gulf of Mexico. Mottled with yellow, white, and brown, it matches these weeds perfectly. It uses its hand-like pectoral fins to pull itself around in the dense clumps of sargassum. **(75)**

Pancake Batfish To 4 in. This Atlantic batfish swims or crawls along the bottom, using its feet-like pectoral fins as oars. It lives from North Carolina south through the Gulf of Mexico. This batfish is reddish brown sprinkled with pale spots and flecks. Its eyes are blue. **(76)**

Goosefish To 4 ft. It is hard for victims to escape this fish's gigantic mouth with its rows of needle-sharp, one-way teeth. It uses its lure-tipped fishing pole in deep Atlantic waters from Quebec south to Florida. It is mottled and flecked with various shades of brown. **(77)**

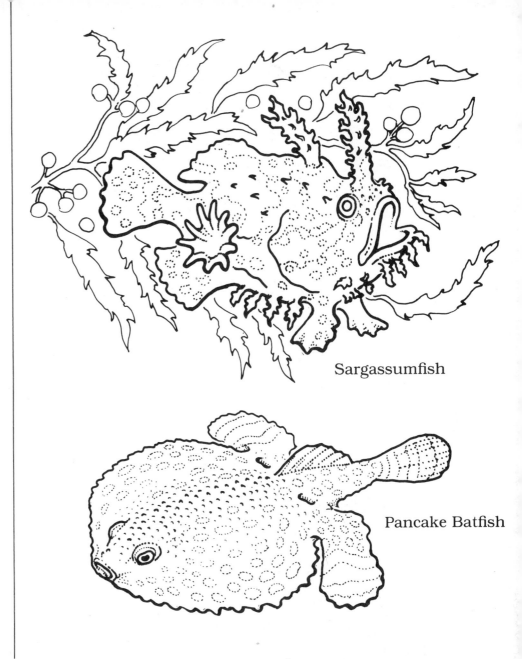

Sargassumfish

Pancake Batfish

Goosefish

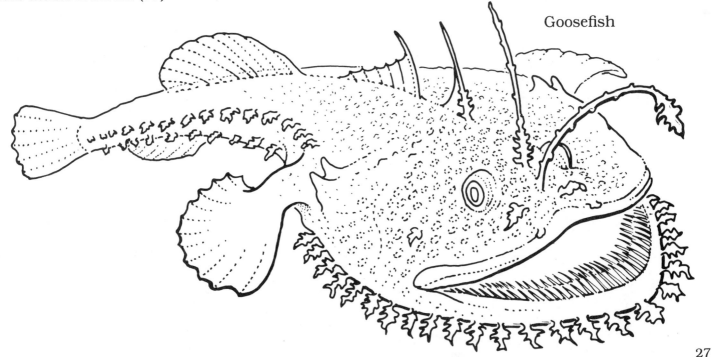

27

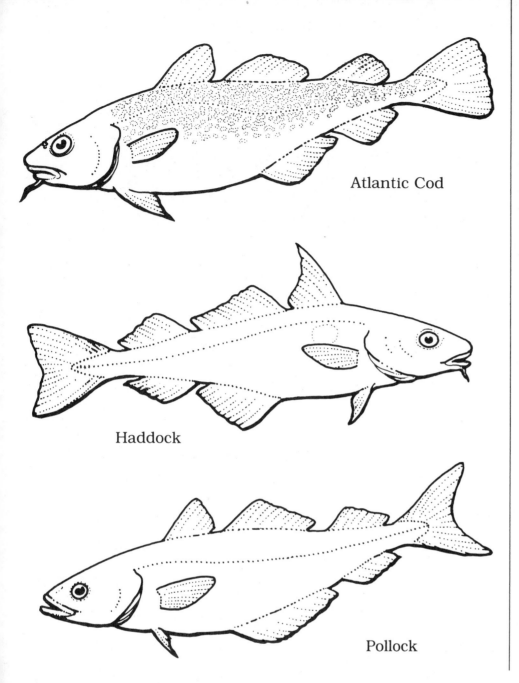

Atlantic Cod

Haddock

Pollock

Cod-like Fishes

The fishes in this well-known marine group are large and tasty and of great commercial importance. As recently as 1958 Iceland and England came close to war over fishing rights.

Atlantic Cod   To 6 ft. These golden, greenish, or reddish fish live in large numbers offshore near the bottom. Cod are found from Greenland south to Cape Hatteras. **(78)**

Haddock   To 3½ ft. This East Coast fish lives in deeper waters than the Cod. It is found from Nova Scotia to Cape Hatteras. It is dark gray above and white below, with a black blotch on its side and a black lateral line. **(79)**

Pollock   To 3½ ft. This cod-like fish lives from the Gulf of St. Lawrence south to New Jersey. It is greenish bronze above, with faintly yellow sides and a white belly. **(80)**

Ocean Pout   To 3½ ft. This cod-like character is well named. A territorial bottom fish, it can be found from the Gulf of St. Lawrence south to Delaware. You have a wide choice of colors: pinkish, yellowish, brownish, or reddish, with darker blotches and a gray belly. **(81)**

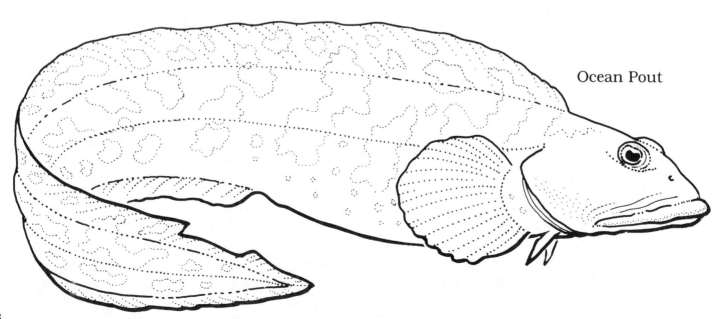

Ocean Pout

River Scene

This group of river fish might be found together in the mid-Mississippi region in clear water with a moderate current. If you like, add more pebbles and plants on the river bed and make the water gradually lighter in color toward the surface. From top to bottom you see: a **Smallmouth Buffalo** (55), a **White Sucker** (61), a **Blue Catfish** (70), and a little **Stonecat** (66).

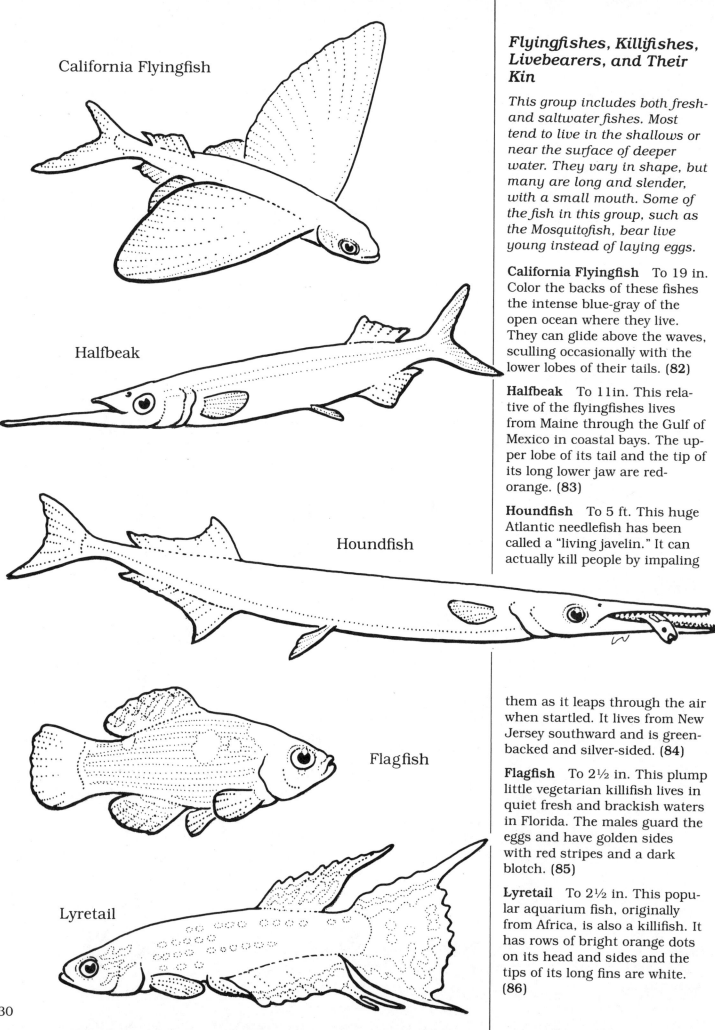

California Flyingfish

Halfbeak

Houndfish

Flagfish

Lyretail

Flyingfishes, Killifishes, Livebearers, and Their Kin

This group includes both fresh- and saltwater fishes. Most tend to live in the shallows or near the surface of deeper water. They vary in shape, but many are long and slender, with a small mouth. Some of the fish in this group, such as the Mosquitofish, bear live young instead of laying eggs.

California Flyingfish To 19 in. Color the backs of these fishes the intense blue-gray of the open ocean where they live. They can glide above the waves, sculling occasionally with the lower lobes of their tails. (82)

Halfbeak To 11 in. This relative of the flyingfishes lives from Maine through the Gulf of Mexico in coastal bays. The upper lobe of its tail and the tip of its long lower jaw are red-orange. (83)

Houndfish To 5 ft. This huge Atlantic needlefish has been called a "living javelin." It can actually kill people by impaling

them as it leaps through the air when startled. It lives from New Jersey southward and is green-backed and silver-sided. (84)

Flagfish To 2½ in. This plump little vegetarian killifish lives in quiet fresh and brackish waters in Florida. The males guard the eggs and have golden sides with red stripes and a dark blotch. (85)

Lyretail To 2½ in. This popular aquarium fish, originally from Africa, is also a killifish. It has rows of bright orange dots on its head and sides and the tips of its long fins are white. (86)

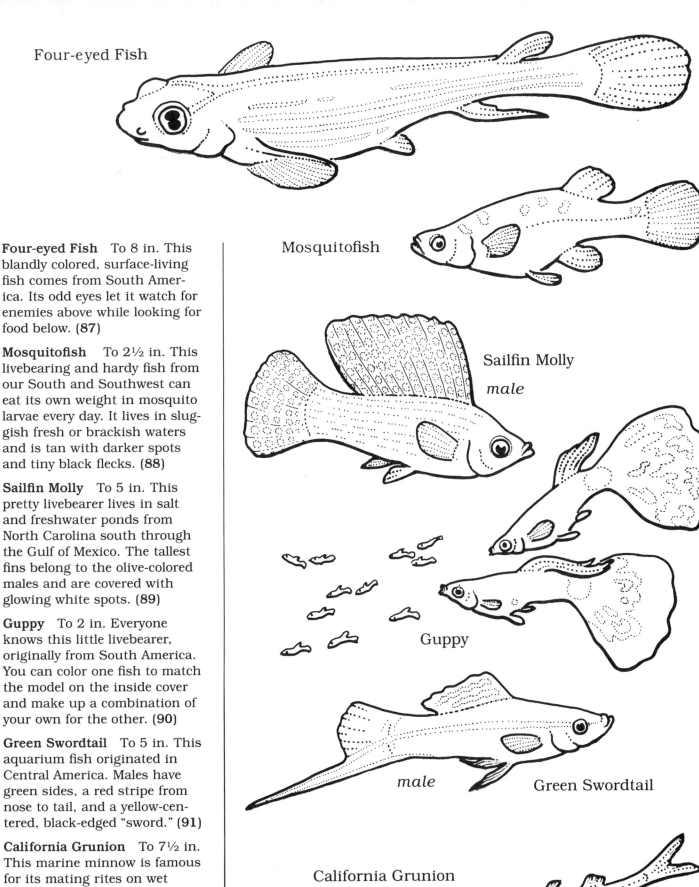

Four-eyed Fish

Mosquitofish

Sailfin Molly
male

Guppy

male Green Swordtail

California Grunion

Four-eyed Fish To 8 in. This blandly colored, surface-living fish comes from South America. Its odd eyes let it watch for enemies above while looking for food below. **(87)**

Mosquitofish To 2½ in. This livebearing and hardy fish from our South and Southwest can eat its own weight in mosquito larvae every day. It lives in sluggish fresh or brackish waters and is tan with darker spots and tiny black flecks. **(88)**

Sailfin Molly To 5 in. This pretty livebearer lives in salt and freshwater ponds from North Carolina south through the Gulf of Mexico. The tallest fins belong to the olive-colored males and are covered with glowing white spots. **(89)**

Guppy To 2 in. Everyone knows this little livebearer, originally from South America. You can color one fish to match the model on the inside cover and make up a combination of your own for the other. **(90)**

Green Swordtail To 5 in. This aquarium fish originated in Central America. Males have green sides, a red stripe from nose to tail, and a yellow-centered, black-edged "sword." **(91)**

California Grunion To 7½ in. This marine minnow is famous for its mating rites on wet beaches during spring and fall high tides. From San Francisco to Baja it spawns by the millions. Give yours a blue-gray back and a thin, glowing, yellow-green line down the sides. **(92)**

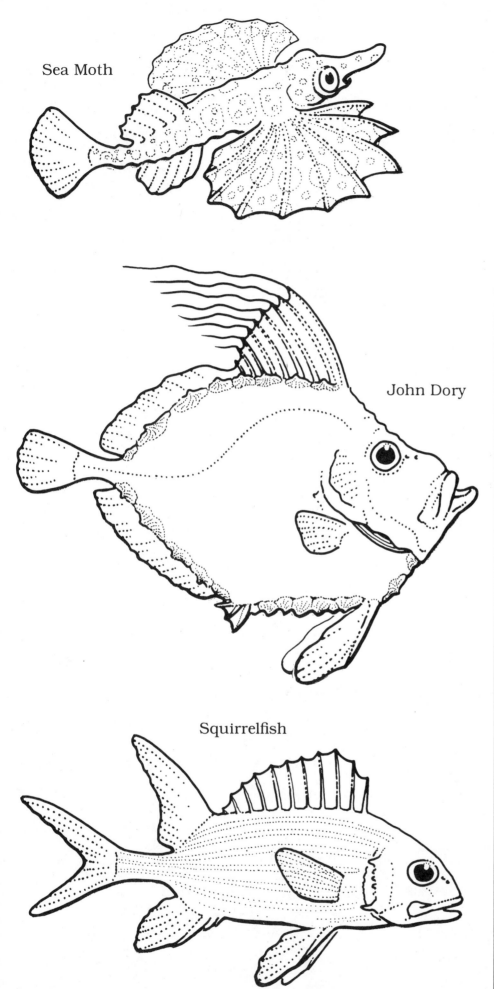

Sea Moth

John Dory

Squirrelfish

Pegasiformes

Like Pegasus, the mythical flying horse, the fishes in this group can "fly," using their tiny, wing-like pectoral fins. These bony-plated marine fishes also have a long, horse-like snout.

Sea Moth   To 5 in. This little mottled brown fish is speckled all over with white. It can be found skittering over the waves in the Indo-Pacific region. **(93)**

Dories

Offshore fishermen are amused when these solitary, big-faced, spiny fishes come aboard in their trawls. These fishes live in the open sea and are seldom seen in aquariums.

John Dory   To 20 in. This silvery Atlantic dory is found from Newfoundland and Georges Bank south to Virginia. **(94)**

Squirrelfishes and Their Kin

Many of the small marine fishes in this group are nocturnal, as you might guess by the size of their eyes. Quite a few are red in color. Some live at great depths and are little known.

Squirrelfish   To 14 in. This fish can be found in deeper water from North Carolina south into the Gulf of Mexico. It has a red head, fainter red stripes on its body, and white, flag-like spots on its dorsal fin. **(95)**

Fangtooth To 6 in. You will probably never meet this fish in person. It is found a third of a mile down, far off of both our North American coasts. It is a fierce little fish and its color is black. (96)

Atlantic Flashlightfish To 5 in. This small black fish lives along steep drop-offs in the West Indies. It has a greenish white light organ under its eye which it can switch on and off. (97)

Fangtooth

Flying Gurnards

The marine fishes in this group use their huge, winglike pectoral fins and fingerlike rays to walk or glide along the bottom where they live. Their heads are encased in a spiny, bony covering.

Atlantic
Flashlightfish

Flying Gurnard

Flying Gurnard To 18 in. In clear coastal waters from Massachusetts south through the Gulf of Mexico this blunt-nosed fish can be found. It has extravagantly beautiful blue- to lavender-spotted, fanlike "wings." (98)

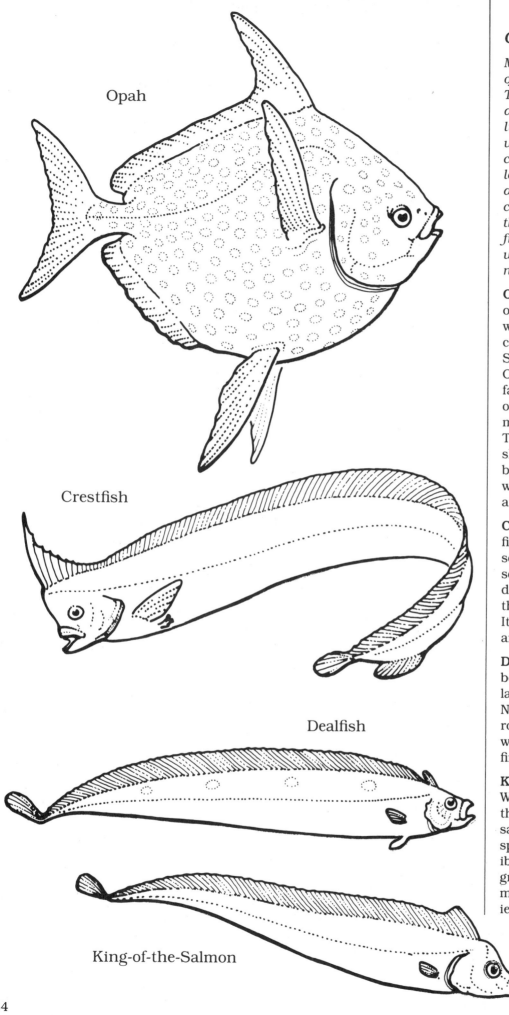

Opah

Crestfish

Dealfish

King-of-the-Salmon

Crestfishes and Their Kin

Most of us will never see any of these spectacular fishes. They resemble creatures from an enchanted fairy tale and live far out at sea in the world's great oceans. All except the Opah have startlingly long, ribbonlike bodies. They all have unusual mouths that can project outward to grab their prey. When a dead fish from this fantastic group is washed ashore, it is always news.

Opah To 5 ft. There is only one Opah. It is found worldwide and off North American coasts from Alaska and Nova Scotia southward. Although Opahs seem rare, they live so far below the surface and so far out to sea that there may be more of them than we think. They are a rich, deep blue, shading to silvery pink on the belly and are covered all over with silver spots. All their fins are crimson. **(99)**

Crestfish To 6 ft. This crestfish is found far at sea from southern California and Florida southward. It lives at great depths and has an ink sac like that of a squid or a cuttlefish. It has a brown and silvery body and red fins. **(100)**

Dealfish To 8½ ft. This ribbonfish lives, sometimes in large groups, far at sea in the North Atlantic. It has a silvery, rough-skinned body, an upward-turned red tail, and red fins. **(101)**

King-of-the-Salmon To 6 ft. When Northwest Indians saw this ribbonfish they knew the salmon were coming home to spawn. Deep-diving submersibles have seen these fish at great depths. Their lives are a mystery. They have silver bodies and crimson fins. **(102)**

Unicornfish To 5 ft. This crestfish lives widely in the world's oceans. Off our coasts it has been seen near Florida. It too has an ink sac. It is silvery with dozens of dark bands on its body and red fins. It is named for the projecting "horn" on its forehead. (**103**)

Unicornfish

Oarfish

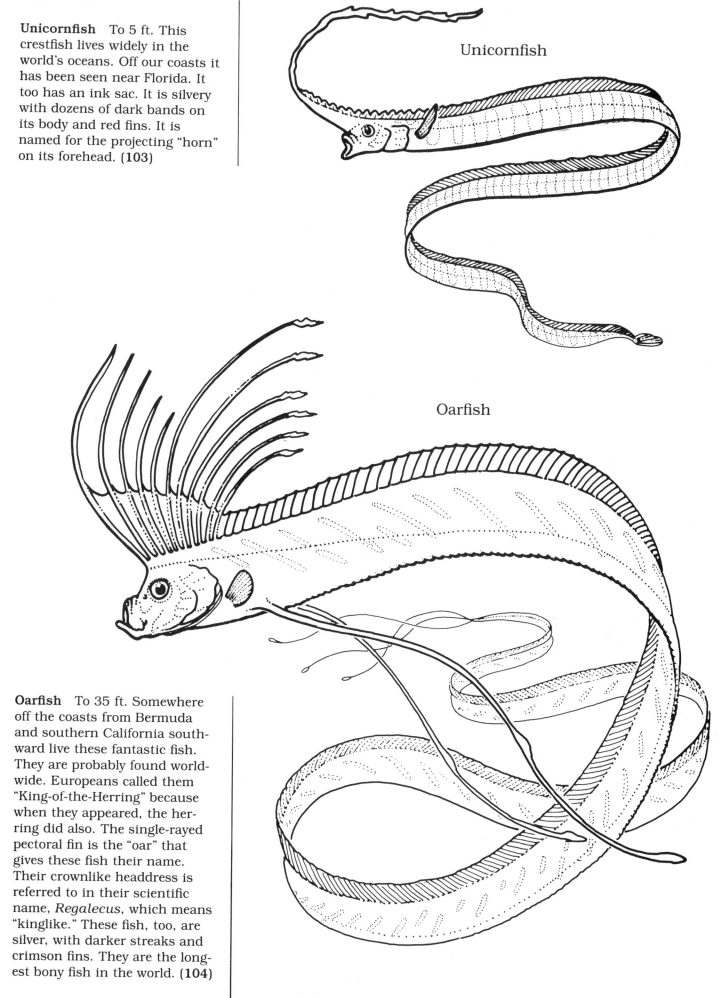

Oarfish To 35 ft. Somewhere off the coasts from Bermuda and southern California southward live these fantastic fish. They are probably found worldwide. Europeans called them "King-of-the-Herring" because when they appeared, the herring did also. The single-rayed pectoral fin is the "oar" that gives these fish their name. Their crownlike headdress is referred to in their scientific name, *Regalecus*, which means "kinglike." These fish, too, are silver, with darker streaks and crimson fins. They are the longest bony fish in the world. (**104**)

35

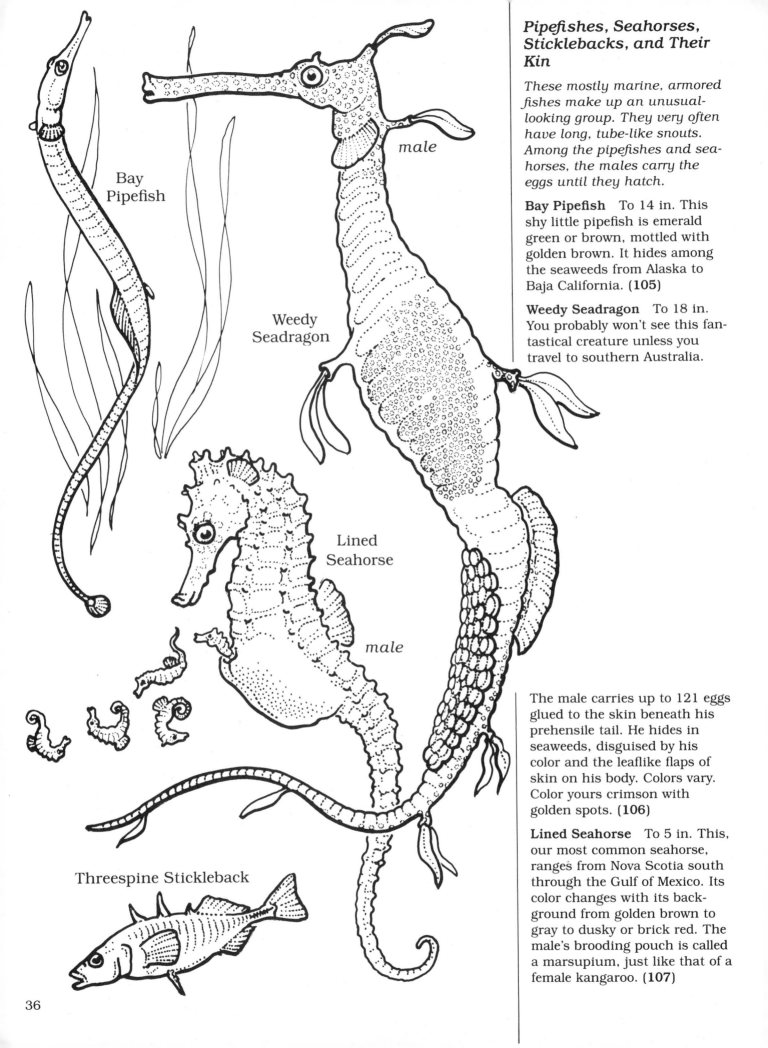

Bay Pipefish

male

Weedy Seadragon

Lined Seahorse

male

Threespine Stickleback

Pipefishes, Seahorses, Sticklebacks, and Their Kin

These mostly marine, armored fishes make up an unusual-looking group. They very often have long, tube-like snouts. Among the pipefishes and seahorses, the males carry the eggs until they hatch.

Bay Pipefish To 14 in. This shy little pipefish is emerald green or brown, mottled with golden brown. It hides among the seaweeds from Alaska to Baja California. (105)

Weedy Seadragon To 18 in. You probably won't see this fantastical creature unless you travel to southern Australia.

The male carries up to 121 eggs glued to the skin beneath his prehensile tail. He hides in seaweeds, disguised by his color and the leaflike flaps of skin on his body. Colors vary. Color yours crimson with golden spots. (106)

Lined Seahorse To 5 in. This, our most common seahorse, ranges from Nova Scotia south through the Gulf of Mexico. Its color changes with its background from golden brown to gray to dusky or brick red. The male's brooding pouch is called a marsupium, just like that of a female kangaroo. (107)

Threespine Stickleback To 4 in. This prickly little fish lives in cool waters — salt, brackish, or fresh — on both coasts. The male guards the female's eggs and hatched young. Usually these fish are gray to golden olive. Why not make yours a breeding male, with a blood-orange body and a bright blue eye? **(108)**

Bluespotted Cornetfish To 5 ft. This startling fish is found in shallow warm waters from Nova Scotia south to the Gulf of Mexico. Like many other members of this fish group, the cornetfish hides by floating vertically to blend in with grasses and seaweeds. The middle rays of this fish's tail form a long filament to add to the effect. Color it greenish brown with rows of light blue spots. **(109)**

Trumpetfish To 30 in. This long but stout fish often hangs head down in the water near tall soft corals. When a meal passes beneath it, the Trumpetfish lunges downwards and slurps it up through its long snout. The Trumpetfish is found from south Florida south through the Gulf of Mexico. It has a dull reddish back with long silvery blue lines and black spots along its sides. **(110)**

Slender Snipefish To 6 in. This pinkish to greenish silvery fish is found worldwide in warm seas near the edges of continental shelves. Snipefish live at the bottom in schools, picking up tiny creatures with their small mouths. On our coasts, they are found from southern California and Florida southward. This fish has rough, sandpaper-like skin. Its young sometimes travel in enormous groups. **(111)**

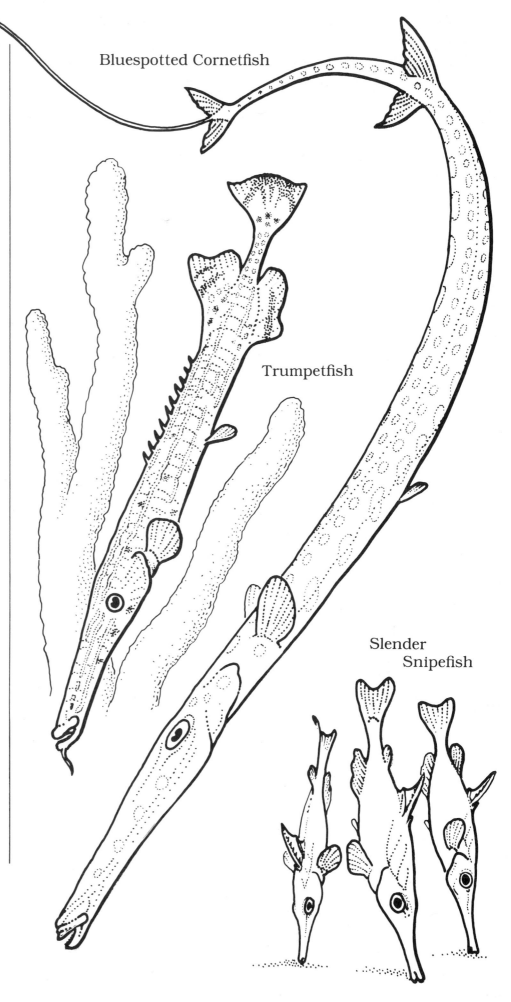

Bluespotted Cornetfish

Trumpetfish

Slender Snipefish

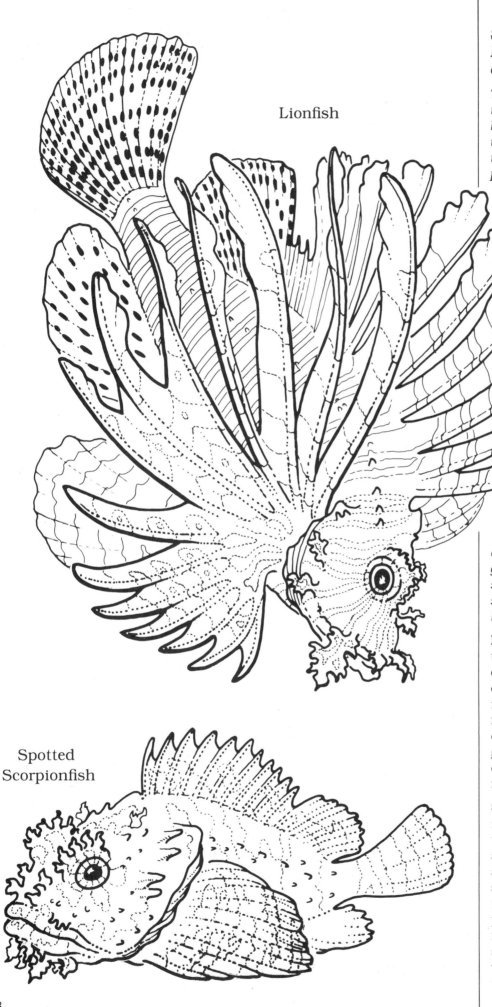

Lionfish

Spotted
Scorpionfish

Scorpionfishes, Rockfishes, Sculpins, and Their Kin

The fishes in this group are mostly marine. Most have bony cheek plates and lots of venomous spines. Some exotic members of this group are so poisonous that one jab can result in excruciating pain, shock, and death.

Even our North American scorpionfishes and rockfishes have poison glands associated with their spines. Though not fatally poisonous, they should all be handled with care.

Lionfish   To 12 in. This beautiful red, black, and white fish of the Indo-Pacific region puts on a breathtaking display with its long pectoral and dorsal fins. This is a warning. Head down, these fishes hustle aggressively toward intruders and can inflict very painful, possibly fatal, wounds. (**112**)

Spotted Scorpionfish   To 17 in. One of our scorpionfishes, this chunky, grumpy-looking animal lives in shallow, rocky areas from Massachusetts south through the Gulf of Mexico. Mottled with gray, black, pink, and green, this fish matches the bottom. It can show its startling black and white armpits to warn that it too is venomous. (**113**)

Redfish (Ocean Perch) To 20 in. You may see the big eyes of this large-headed, golden and rosy rockfish staring at you from atop a pile of crushed ice in the supermarkets, where it is marketed as Ocean Perch. It lives along the East Coast from Greenland to New Jersey. **(114)**

China Rockfish To 17 in. There are many handsome West Coast rockfishes. This one is blue-black mottled with lighter blue. A bold yellow marking extends from its spiny dorsal fin to its tail. It is found from Alaska to mid-California. **(115)**

Kelp Poacher To 3½ in. This brightly colored and jolly little poacher lives among the rocks from British Columbia to Central California. It is red and white and its body is covered with flaps of skin, bits of sponge, and seaweed. **(116)**

Quillback Rockfish To 24 in. This rockfish ranges from Alaska to Point Conception, California, and is notable for its especially long spines. Color the head and back yellowish. **(117)**

The shrimp below is pink. **(117)**

Smooth Skeleton Shrimp

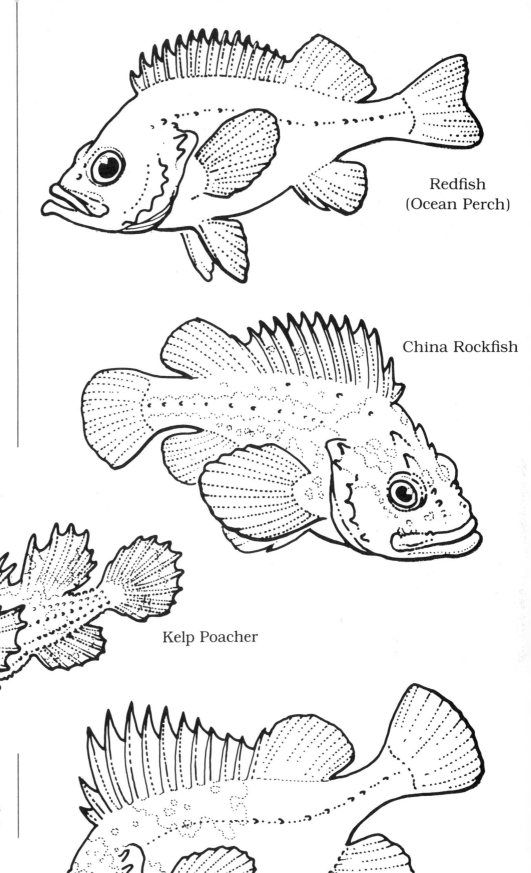

Redfish (Ocean Perch)

China Rockfish

Kelp Poacher

Quillback Rockfish

Bighead Searobin

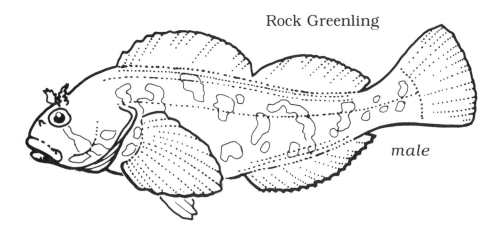

Rock Greenling

male

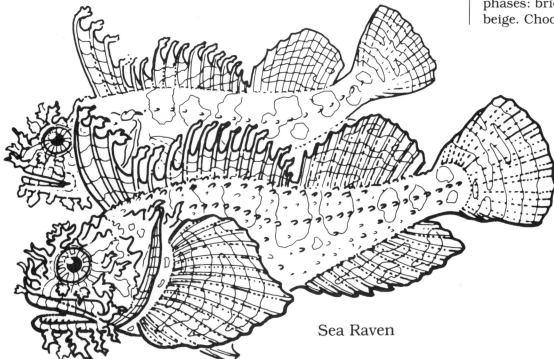

Sea Raven

Scorpionfishes and Their Kin, *continued*

Bighead Searobin   To 14 in. This Atlantic searobin with a large, spiny head is common in sheltered water near shore, from the Chesapeake south through the Gulf of Mexico. Its large, winglike pectoral fins are pale yellow, narrowly striped with black. (**118**)

Rock Greenling   To 2 ft. The mouth of this Pacific Coast greenling is often blue inside. The body is greenish brown. Males are strongly marked with red patches and red edges to their fins. Greenlings are colorful. Unlike other members of the scorpionfish group, they have smooth heads. Many, like this one, have fringed "eyebrows." The Rock Greenling is found from the Bering Sea south to Point Conception, California. (**119**)

Sea Raven   To 25 in. This big, fringed sculpin lives among weeds and rocks from Labrador south to the Chesapeake. Like other fishes in this group, it is a bottom fish, and uses its big, fleshy pectoral fins to crawl along the bottom. This fish comes in three mottled color phases: brick red, yellow, or beige. Choose two. (**120**)

Lumpfish To 23 in. This chunky lumpfish is studded with tubercles, like the studs on a dog's armored collar. It lives over rocks along the Atlantic Coast from Hudson's Bay south to the Chesapeake. This fish has a ventral sucking disc, which helps it hold onto rocks in the current. The Lumpfish is bluish, brownish, reddish, or yellowish when adult and lime green when young. Its masses of eggs make delicious caviar. (**121**)

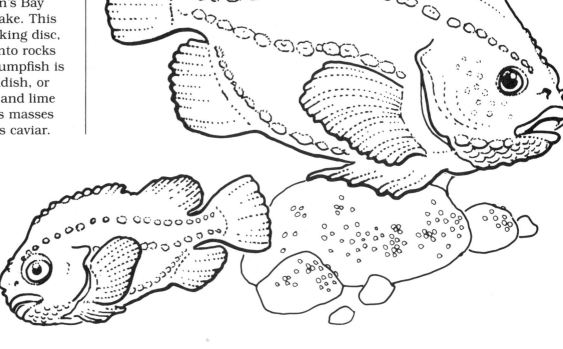

Lumpfish

Banded Sculpin

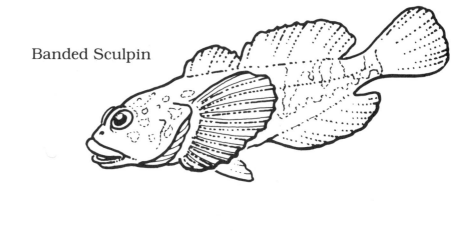

Banded Sculpin To 5 in. This fleshy-lipped reddish brown or olive-gray sculpin lives in fresh water. It likes clean creeks and rivers in the central southeastern states. The somewhat upward-gazing eyes show that it too is a bottom fish. (**122**)

Red Irish Lord To 20 in. This colorful character is red, brown, and white with black mottling. It is commonly found in intertidal areas from the Bering Sea south to Monterey on the California coast. (**123**)

Red Irish Lord

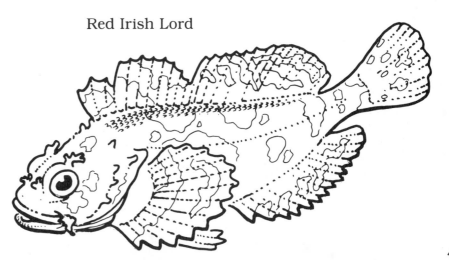

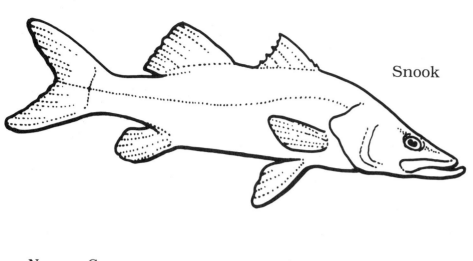

Snook

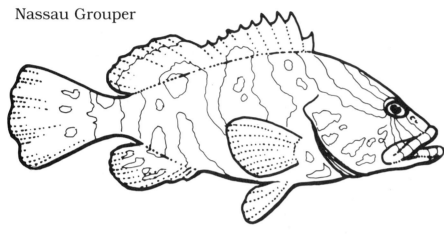

Nassau Grouper

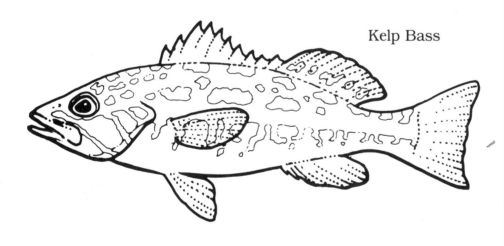

Kelp Bass

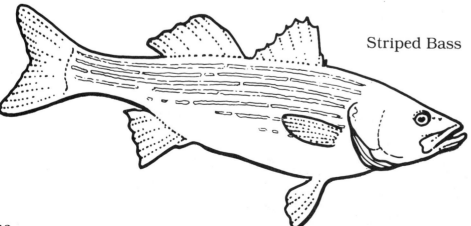

Striped Bass

Perch-like Fishes

This huge and successful group is the largest order, not only of fishes but of all vertebrates. These fishes are found worldwide in salt and fresh water. The forward parts of their dorsal and anal fins have spines. For this reason they are called spiny-rayed fishes. They have a classic "fishy" look. All the fishes shown on the next 18 pages (pp. 42–59) belong to this large group.

Snook To 4½ ft. This sleek and fast snook lives in shallow coastal waters from North Carolina south to the Gulf of Mexico. It is pale greenish gray above and silvery white below, with a black lateral line extending to the tip of its tail. It is an excellent sport fish, but beware — its sharp gill covers can cut you. **(124)**

Nassau Grouper To 4 ft. This handsome sea bass is usually brown and tan. It always has a dark blotch at the base of its tail and lines radiating from its eyes. Solitary but tame, it often allows divers to approach. It lives on the East Coast from North Carolina south to the Gulf of Mexico. **(125)**

Kelp Bass To 28 in. This West Coast sea bass lives in kelp beds and shipwrecks from the Columbia River south to Baja California. A good and tasty sport fish, it is golden brown above, with a white belly and white blotches along its sides. **(126)**

Striped Bass To 6 ft. This bass is growing rarer through too much popularity. It feeds in schools along the coast from the St. Lawrence River south to North Florida. It is light gray with a white belly, dusky fins, and numerous dark horizontal stripes. **(127)**

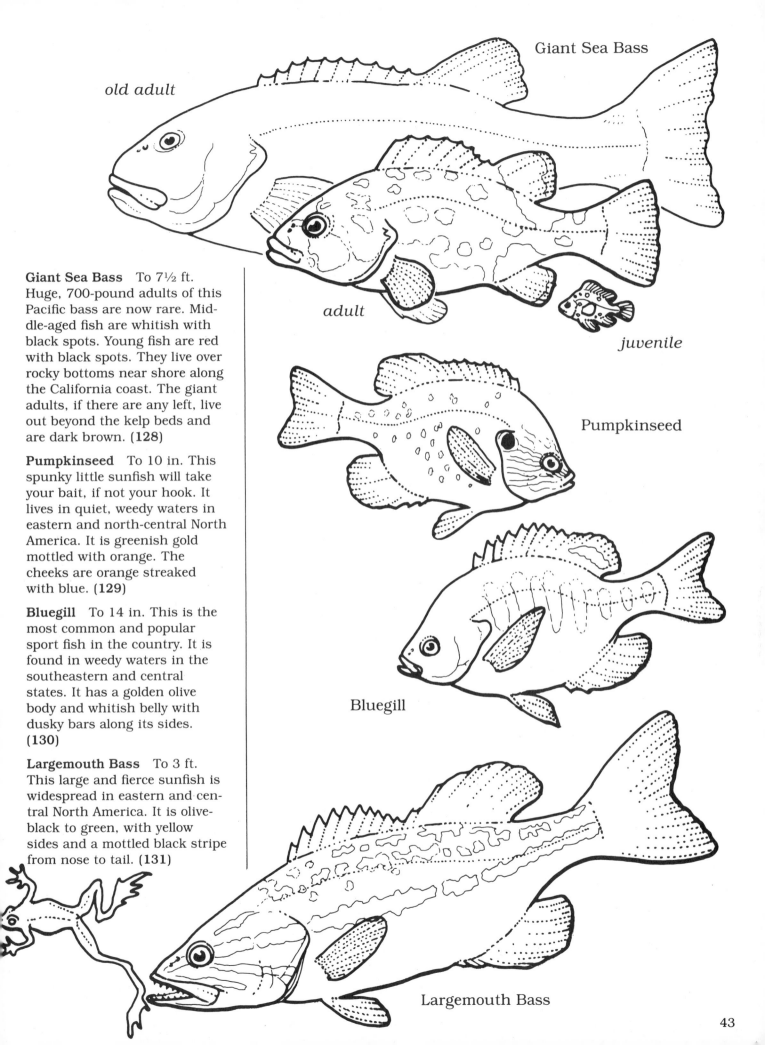

Giant Sea Bass

old adult

adult

juvenile

Pumpkinseed

Bluegill

Largemouth Bass

Giant Sea Bass To 7½ ft. Huge, 700-pound adults of this Pacific bass are now rare. Middle-aged fish are whitish with black spots. Young fish are red with black spots. They live over rocky bottoms near shore along the California coast. The giant adults, if there are any left, live out beyond the kelp beds and are dark brown. **(128)**

Pumpkinseed To 10 in. This spunky little sunfish will take your bait, if not your hook. It lives in quiet, weedy waters in eastern and north-central North America. It is greenish gold mottled with orange. The cheeks are orange streaked with blue. **(129)**

Bluegill To 14 in. This is the most common and popular sport fish in the country. It is found in weedy waters in the southeastern and central states. It has a golden olive body and whitish belly with dusky bars along its sides. **(130)**

Largemouth Bass To 3 ft. This large and fierce sunfish is widespread in eastern and central North America. It is olive-black to green, with yellow sides and a mottled black stripe from nose to tail. **(131)**

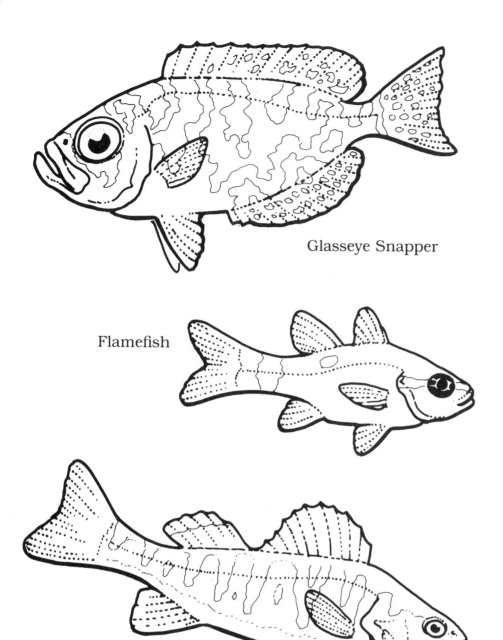

Glasseye Snapper

Flamefish

Yellow Perch

More Perch-like Fishes

Glasseye Snapper To 15 in. The large eyes of this fish suggest its partially nocturnal habits. It is silver, marbled and blotched with red. It lives along the East Coast from New Jersey south through the Gulf of Mexico. (**132**)

Flamefish To 4 in. This member of the cardinalfish family is common in shallow water along sea walls and over rubble and reefs from Florida south along the Gulf Coast. It is often seen in marine aquariums. It is deep orange-red with a black spot on its body, a black saddle-mark on its tail, and a tiny black spot on its gill cover. (**133**)

Yellow Perch To 15 in. This perch belongs to a large freshwater family and is found widely east of the Rockies. It is brownish yellow above with bright yellow sides and dark bars. It has faintly orange lower fins in breeding season. (**134**)

Walleye To 3½ ft. This is the largest North American perch. It is found in the north-central states in lakes with clear water and hard bottoms. The Walleye is golden brown or green above with a faintly greenish white belly. The lower tip of its tail fin is also white. It is a highly valued sports fish. (**135**)

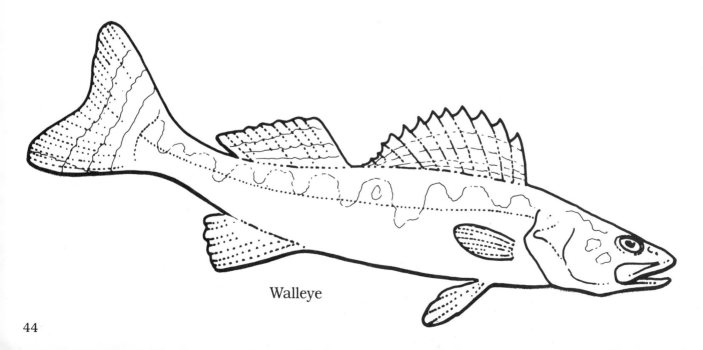

Walleye

Rainbow Darter To 3 in. This exquisitely beautiful little perch is one of many pretty darters in North America. It lives over gravel and rocks in fast, clear creeks and rivers in the central states. Water pollution threatens darters, as it does many native fish, because they need clean, well-aerated water. The name of this darter describes its colors. Start with a blue-green edge on the dorsal fin and refer to the inside back cover for the rest of the rainbow. (136)

Tilefish To 3½ ft. This deepwater marine fish used to be caught in vast numbers from Nova Scotia south into the Gulf of Mexico. A beautiful but odd-looking fish, it too has all the colors of a rainbow. Start with its bluish to greenish back and add yellow spots. Note the spotted stripe along its dorsal fin. (137)

Ocean Whitefish To 3 ft. This Pacific tilefish is also beautifully colored. It lives offshore from Vancouver Island south to Peru. Be sure to add brilliant blue edges to all the fins and to the edge of its gill cover. (138)

Bluefish To 3½ ft. Bluefish are impressive, voracious predators. They feed in schools from Nova Scotia south through the Gulf of Mexico. They are a good-tasting, dark-fleshed fish. Don't swim near a feeding school. In a feeding frenzy they can confuse your fingers and toes with food. (139)

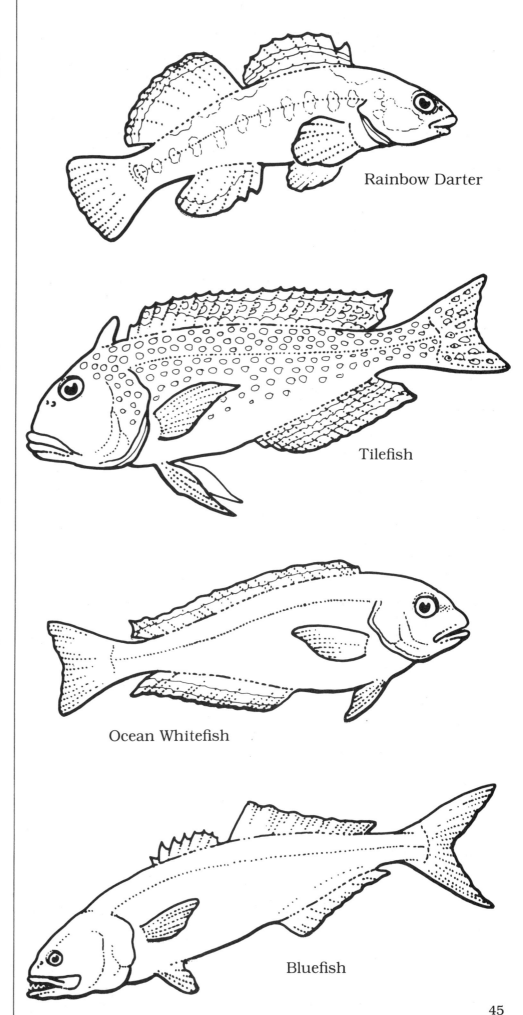

Rainbow Darter

Tilefish

Ocean Whitefish

Bluefish

45

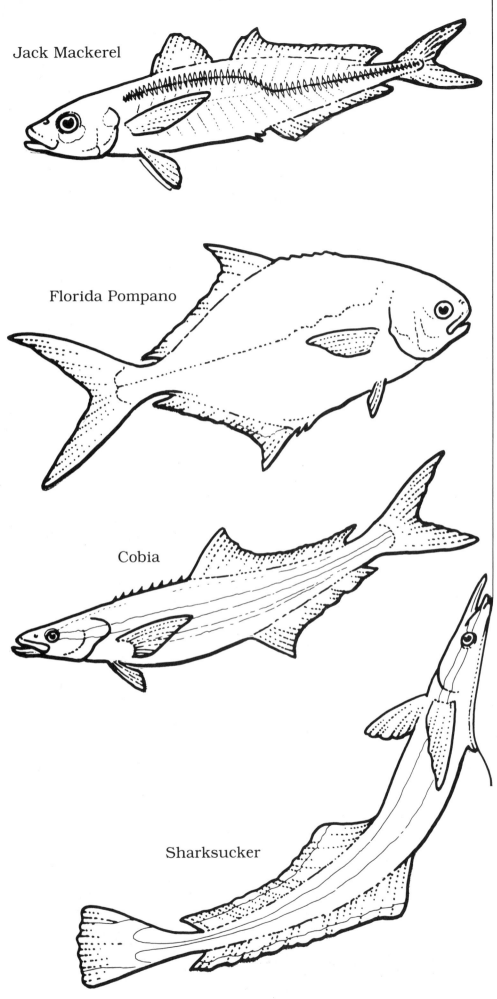

Jack Mackerel

Florida Pompano

Cobia

Sharksucker

More Perch-like Fishes

Jack Mackerel To 32 in. This silvery jack with a dark spot on its gill cover is found in large schools from Alaska to Baja California. It has bony plates called scutes all along its lateral line. Sea lions as well as people find it good eating. (**140**)

Florida Pompano To 17 in. This fast, blunt-nosed jack can be found in the Atlantic from Massachusetts southward into the Gulf of Mexico. It is a lively fighter and a popular game fish. It is blue-gray or green, with silvery sides and often has some yellow on its belly. (**141**)

Cobia To 6½ ft. There is only one cobia. It is found in open seas worldwide and on our East Coast from the mid-Atlantic states southward. Like the remoras, it associates with larger fish to pick up their food scraps. Unlike a remora, it has no suction disc on its head; instead, it has a row of short, sharp spines. The Cobia is dark brown above, with two bright white stripes surrounding a black line. Its belly is a warm gray. (**142**)

Sharksucker To 32 in. This remora is found worldwide in warm oceans except along the Pacific Coast. Like other remoras, it has a suction disc on its head. It is not particular; it will attach itself to sharks, other fishes, turtles, or even bathers. Its body color varies somewhat — why not color your fish slate blue above and below, with a black stripe at midside, set off by two white stripes. (**143**)

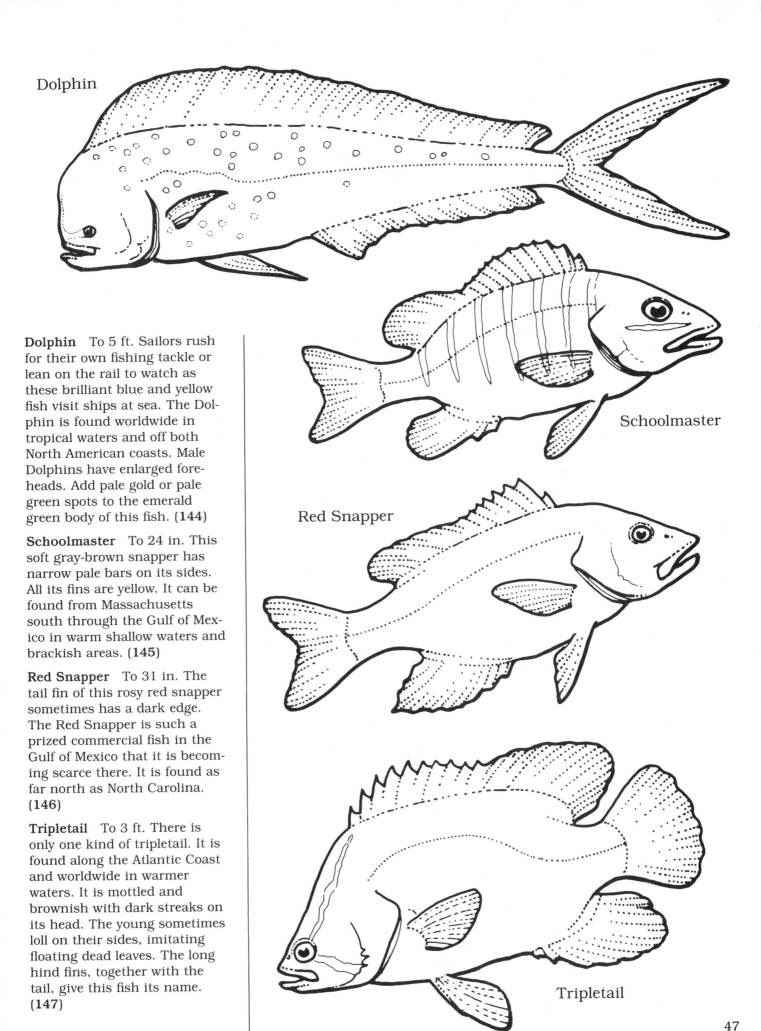

Dolphin

Schoolmaster

Red Snapper

Tripletail

Dolphin   To 5 ft. Sailors rush for their own fishing tackle or lean on the rail to watch as these brilliant blue and yellow fish visit ships at sea. The Dolphin is found worldwide in tropical waters and off both North American coasts. Male Dolphins have enlarged foreheads. Add pale gold or pale green spots to the emerald green body of this fish. **(144)**

Schoolmaster   To 24 in. This soft gray-brown snapper has narrow pale bars on its sides. All its fins are yellow. It can be found from Massachusetts south through the Gulf of Mexico in warm shallow waters and brackish areas. **(145)**

Red Snapper   To 31 in. The tail fin of this rosy red snapper sometimes has a dark edge. The Red Snapper is such a prized commercial fish in the Gulf of Mexico that it is becoming scarce there. It is found as far north as North Carolina. **(146)**

Tripletail   To 3 ft. There is only one kind of tripletail. It is found along the Atlantic Coast and worldwide in warmer waters. It is mottled and brownish with dark streaks on its head. The young sometimes loll on their sides, imitating floating dead leaves. The long hind fins, together with the tail, give this fish its name. **(147)**

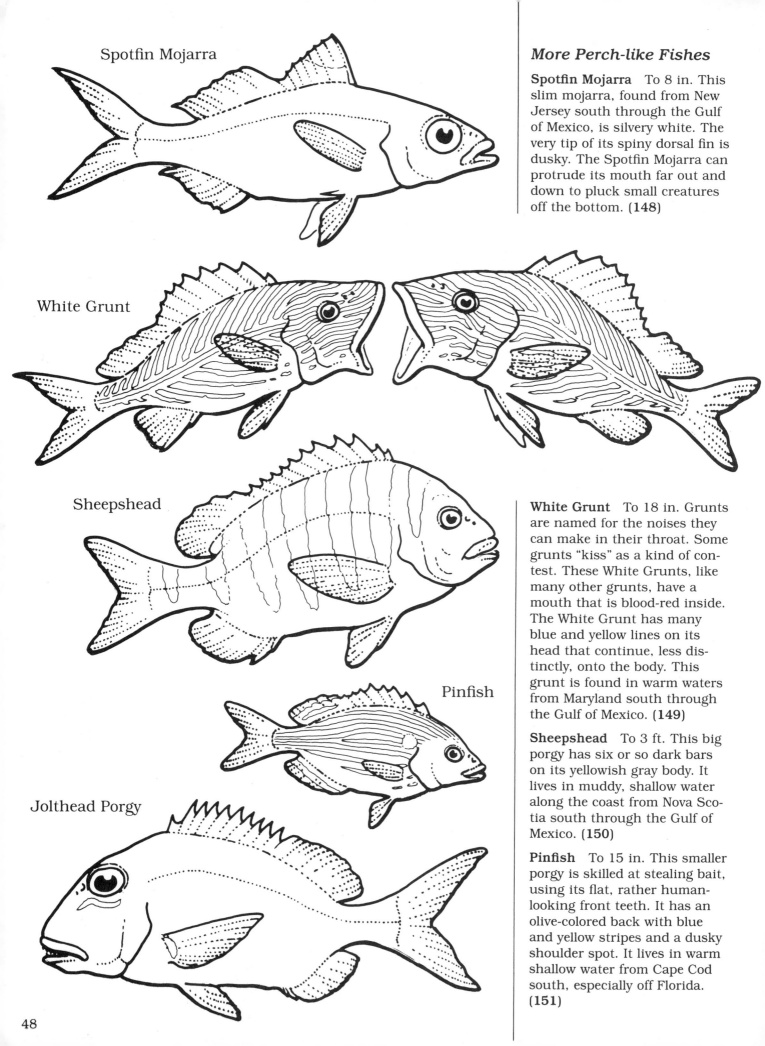

Spotfin Mojarra

White Grunt

Sheepshead

Pinfish

Jolthead Porgy

More Perch-like Fishes

Spotfin Mojarra To 8 in. This slim mojarra, found from New Jersey south through the Gulf of Mexico, is silvery white. The very tip of its spiny dorsal fin is dusky. The Spotfin Mojarra can protrude its mouth far out and down to pluck small creatures off the bottom. **(148)**

White Grunt To 18 in. Grunts are named for the noises they can make in their throat. Some grunts "kiss" as a kind of contest. These White Grunts, like many other grunts, have a mouth that is blood-red inside. The White Grunt has many blue and yellow lines on its head that continue, less distinctly, onto the body. This grunt is found in warm waters from Maryland south through the Gulf of Mexico. **(149)**

Sheepshead To 3 ft. This big porgy has six or so dark bars on its yellowish gray body. It lives in muddy, shallow water along the coast from Nova Scotia south through the Gulf of Mexico. **(150)**

Pinfish To 15 in. This smaller porgy is skilled at stealing bait, using its flat, rather human-looking front teeth. It has an olive-colored back with blue and yellow stripes and a dusky shoulder spot. It lives in warm shallow water from Cape Cod south, especially off Florida. **(151)**

Jolthead Porgy To 2 ft. This big porgy is found from Rhode Island south through the Gulf of Mexico. It has a blue line under its eye and a touch of purple in the corners of its mouth. It crushes mollusks with its large strong teeth. (**152**)

Red Drum To 5 ft. This big drum lives in surf zones from New York south to the Gulf of Mexico. It is coppery gray with one or two pale-rimmed black spots on its tail. As on all drums, the lateral line runs to the tip of the tail. (**153**)

Freshwater Drum To 35 in. This is the only freshwater drum in North America. It is found in the central United States. It is bluish gray above and white below. It can make a drumming noise by vibrating its muscles and using its swim bladder as a sounding box. (**154**)

Jackknife-fish To 9 in. From South Carolina through the Gulf of Mexico, this perky little black-and-white drum is found over rubble or mud in shallow water. Its radical coloration and odd shape probably make this fish harder for other fishes to see. (**155**)

Red Goatfish To 8 in. This pretty goatfish lives in coastal waters from Cape Cod south through the Gulf of Mexico. It is blotched with red and white and has yellow stripes mixed in along its sides. Like other goatfishes, the Red Goatfish uses its chin barbels to probe busily in the bottom for food. (**156**)

Opaleye To 26 in. This fish lives in shallow waters around rocks and kelp in the Pacific from Washington to Baja California. It is olive or gray-green with several white spots on its body and a bright blue eye. Some fish — why not yours? — have white bars across the snout. (**157**)

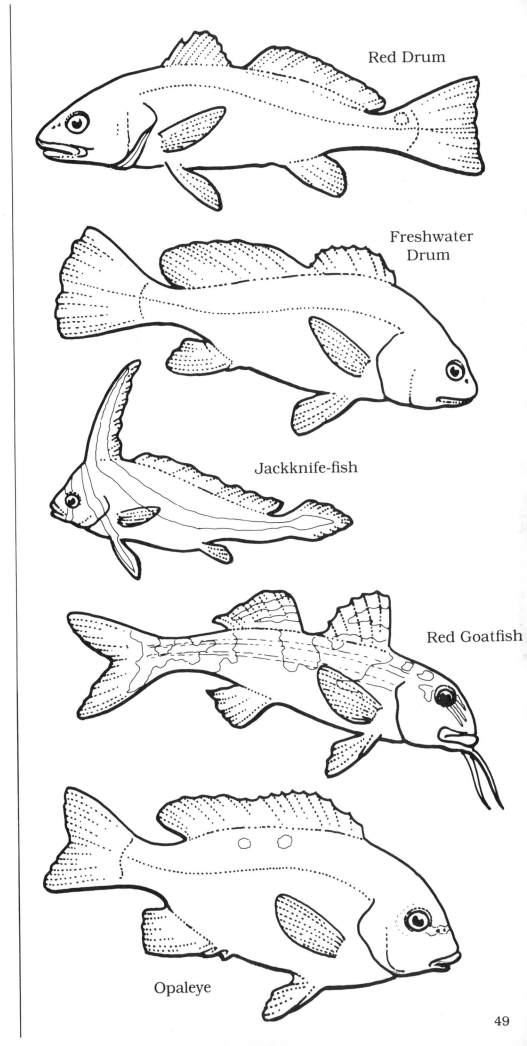

Red Drum

Freshwater Drum

Jackknife-fish

Red Goatfish

Opaleye

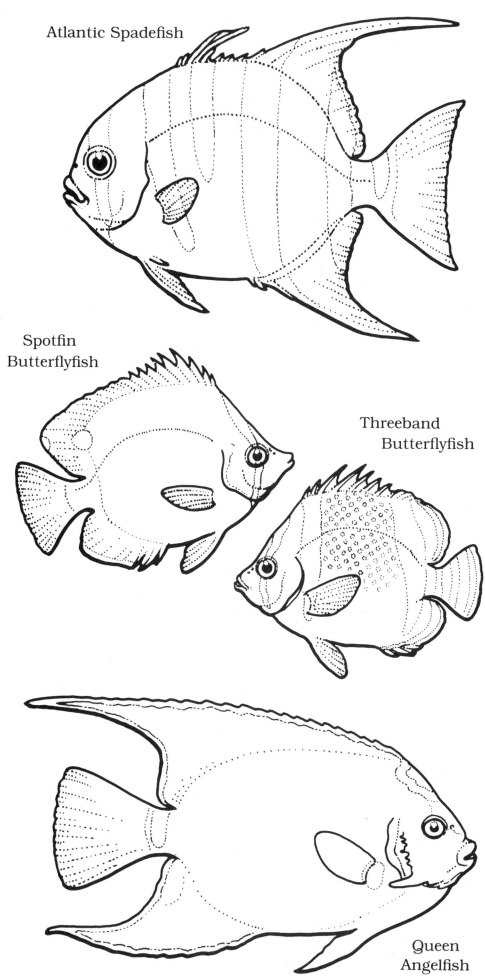

Atlantic Spadefish

Spotfin
Butterflyfish

Threeband
Butterflyfish

Queen
Angelfish

More Perch-like Fishes

Atlantic Spadefish   To 3 ft. The large, disc-shaped spade-fishes travel in schools in warm-ish waters on both coasts. Both the Atlantic and Pacific species are silvery beige with bold black bars on their bodies. They are curious fishes and will some-times encircle divers. They are often associated with wrecked ships. The Atlantic Spadefish, shown here, has longer fins than its Pacific cousin. (**158**)

Spotfin Butterflyfish   To 8 in. This East Coast butterflyfish, like all butterflyfishes, is pretty. It lives in southern waters and into the Gulf of Mexico. It has a white body with yellow fins and a dusky spot. If you want to make yours a male, make the tiny dark spot outlined on the rear edge of the dorsal fin black. (**159**)

Threeband Butterflyfish   To 10 in. This uncommon Pacific Coast butterflyfish is found in rocky areas from San Diego south. It is white, with three dusky bands on the tail and more on the body. (**160**)

Queen Angelfish   To 10 in. This gorgeous angelfish is found from north Florida through the Gulf of Mexico southward. Its most distinctive mark is a bright blue-edged dark patch of scales on its fore-head. Its body is a rich blend of blue and yellow. Actually, *each scale* on the side of this fish is blue with a yellow edge. Refer to photographs in other books if you would like to attempt this coloring feat. Otherwise, just copy the general colors shown in the color picture on the inside back cover. (**161**)

Redtail Surfperch   To 16 in. This surfperch is found from Vancouver Island south to Monterey, California. Commercial fishermen and sportfishermen fish for it along exposed sandy beaches. It is a silvery fish with reddish fins and faint, narrow reddish lines on its body. **(162)**

Striped Surfperch   To 15 in. Surfperches are common on the West Coast. This orange and blue-striped fish lives in surf zones and kelp all along the coast. Unlike most fishes, it gives birth to a small number of surprisingly large young. **(163)**

Rio Grande Cichlid   To 12 in. Cichlids are freshwater fishes that are abundant in the tropics. We have only one native species in North America. You may color the body of this Texas cichlid a medium gray with hundreds of yellow or light blue spots. If you don't feel like trying this, just color it gray and remember the spots. **(164)**

Angelfish   To 6 in. This South American cichlid is a common and peaceful aquarium fish. You can tell it is a cichlid by its single nostrils (most fish have a pair on each side) and its interrupted lateral line. It is silvery brown with dark bars and a lighter belly. **(165)**

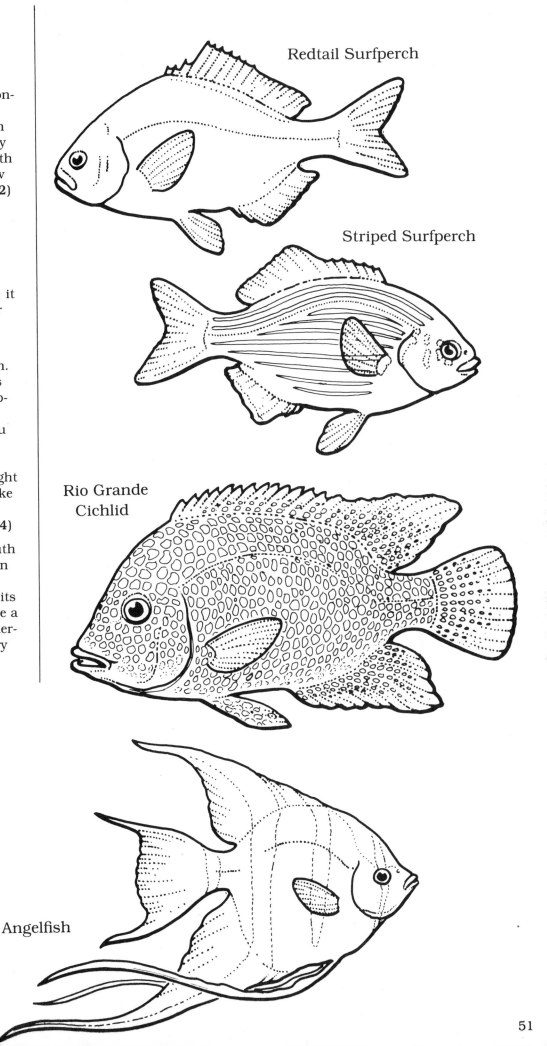

Redtail Surfperch

Striped Surfperch

Rio Grande Cichlid

Angelfish

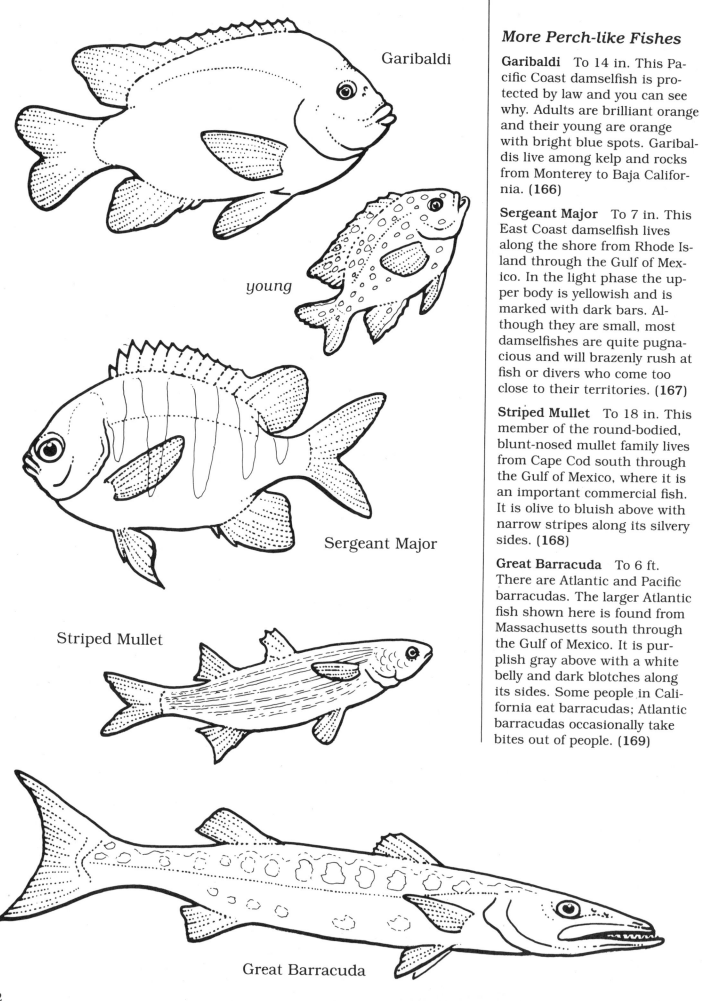

Garibaldi

young

Sergeant Major

Striped Mullet

Great Barracuda

More Perch-like Fishes

Garibaldi To 14 in. This Pacific Coast damselfish is protected by law and you can see why. Adults are brilliant orange and their young are orange with bright blue spots. Garibaldis live among kelp and rocks from Monterey to Baja California. (166)

Sergeant Major To 7 in. This East Coast damselfish lives along the shore from Rhode Island through the Gulf of Mexico. In the light phase the upper body is yellowish and is marked with dark bars. Although they are small, most damselfishes are quite pugnacious and will brazenly rush at fish or divers who come too close to their territories. (167)

Striped Mullet To 18 in. This member of the round-bodied, blunt-nosed mullet family lives from Cape Cod south through the Gulf of Mexico, where it is an important commercial fish. It is olive to bluish above with narrow stripes along its silvery sides. (168)

Great Barracuda To 6 ft. There are Atlantic and Pacific barracudas. The larger Atlantic fish shown here is found from Massachusetts south through the Gulf of Mexico. It is purplish gray above with a white belly and dark blotches along its sides. Some people in California eat barracudas; Atlantic barracudas occasionally take bites out of people. (169)

Slippery Dick To 9 in. Wrasses are alert and curious. This busy little wrasse is common from North Carolina south through the Gulf of Mexico. It has the bucktoothed look characteristic of a wrasse and is a rainbow of pastel colors with two dark stripes from head to tail. **(170)**

California Sheephead To 3 ft. From Monterey to Baja California, this wrasse lives among rocks and kelp beds. The male has a big slate-gray head, a white chin, a brick-red body and a slate gray tail section. This fish also has big front teeth and a wise expression. **(171)**

Tautog To 3 ft. This large East Coast wrasse lives from Nova Scotia to South Carolina around wrecks and piers, where it is often caught. The Tautog is not an exciting color. Take your choice of dull mottled tones. **(172)**

Blue Parrotfish To 4 ft. Blue Parrotfish are occasionally found as far north as Maryland, but prefer warmer waters with coral reefs. Using their strong front teeth, they graze on the algae growing on the reefs and often swallow small pieces of coral at the same time. Much of the "sand" on tropical beaches has passed through the intestines of parrotfishes. You will seldom see these fish in aquariums because they are such specialized feeders and graze on their own exhibit backgrounds until there is nothing left. Color this fish an intense medium blue. Each big, plate-like scale along the sides of this parrotfish actually has a faint pinkish glaze over the center. After you've colored your fish blue, you can go over these scales with pink (see inside back cover) and you will create a very similar effect. **(173)**

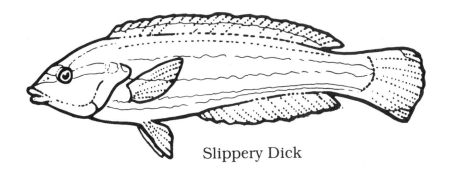

Slippery Dick

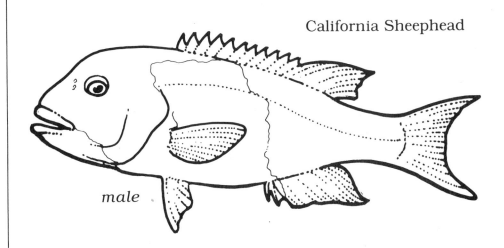

California Sheephead

male

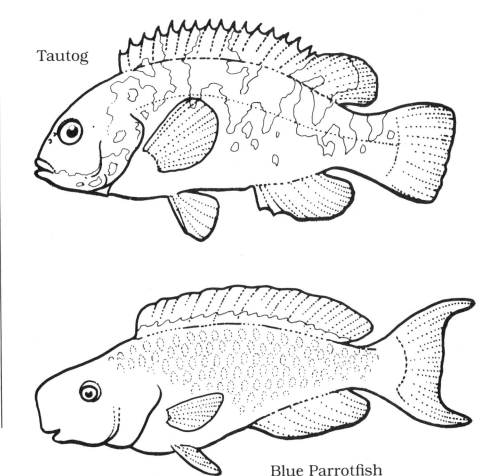

Tautog

Blue Parrotfish

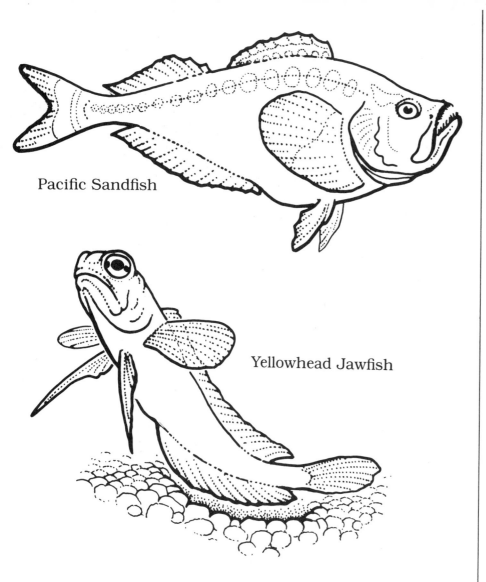

Pacific Sandfish

Yellowhead Jawfish

Barred Blenny

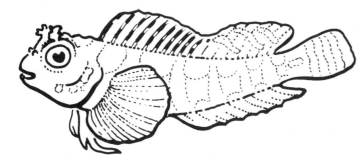

More Perch-like Fishes

Pacific Sandfish   To 12 in. This fish is found in the north Pacific, from the Bering Sea to San Francisco. It is scaleless and dusky colored with darker patches along its back. It buries itself in the mud or sand and waits for prey to blunder into its fringed open mouth. **(174)**

Yellowhead Jawfish   To 4 in. Popular in marine aquariums because they are always busy digging holes or defending them. This blue-bodied, yellow-headed, large-jawed fish is found from south Florida southward. **(175)**

Barred Blenny   To 4 in. Jaunty little blennies of many kinds are found on both coasts of North America. This one lives amid rubble and coral reefs off Florida and southward. It has a yellow-brown body with six dark side bars. **(176)**

Southern Stargazer   To 17 in. Lucky we are to live on the same planet with something as beautifully ugly as this fish. It lies buried in sand, waiting for prey to come near its huge mouth. For added punch, it can produce an electric charge using special organs behind its eyes. It is dark above, sprinkled all over with white spots. It lives near shore from North Carolina south through the Gulf of Mexico. **(177)**

Southern Stargazer

Giant Kelpfish To 2 ft. This slender, long-snouted fish lives among the kelp from British Columbia south to Baja California. Its body color matches its background. As it sways with the waves surging among the kelp, it is almost invisible. Color it either olive-green or reddish brown, with darker broken stripes. (**178**)

Monkeyface Prickleback To 2½ ft. This lumpy-looking fish has a funny face as an adult. Its prickly dorsal fin is encased in flesh. This prickleback lives from Oregon to Baja California. It is grayish, sometimes with dull orange spots on the body and orange edges on the fins. (**179**)

Atlantic Wolffish To 5 ft. This impressively ugly fish lives from Greenland to Cape Cod. It has a powerful bite and can be quite dangerous. Even in heavy boots, fishermen are wary of stepping near these fish when they accidentally come aboard in trawls. Most Wolffish are slate gray with dark, mottled bars along the body. (**180**)

Wolf-eel To 7 ft. This long Pacific wolffish lives in crevices on rocky bottoms along the coast from Alaska to San Diego. It is beige-gray with dark spots outlined with white. Its strong jaws will chomp on anything, including people, but it normally dines on sea urchins, crabs, and snails. (**181**)

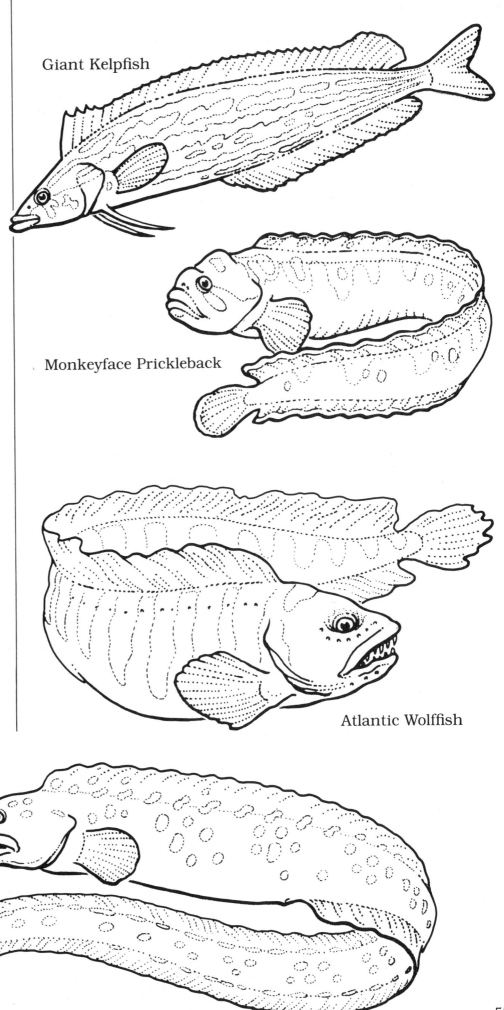

Giant Kelpfish

Monkeyface Prickleback

Atlantic Wolffish

Wolf-eel

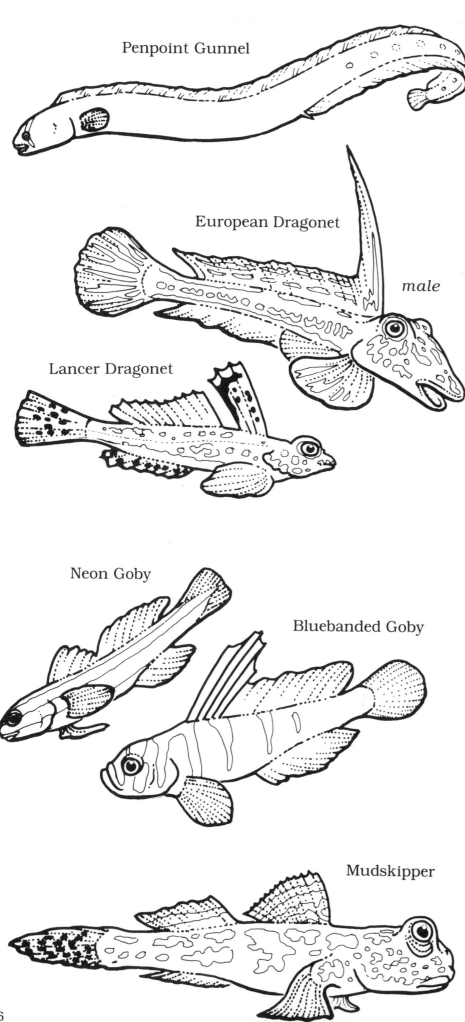

Penpoint Gunnel

European Dragonet

male

Lancer Dragonet

Neon Goby

Bluebanded Goby

Mudskipper

More Perch-like Fishes

Penpoint Gunnel To 18 in. This slim fish lives from Alaska to southern California in shallow waters along the coast. Its name comes from the strong little spine at the front of its anal fin. Take your choice of colors: green, light brown, red, or yellow, with a row of white dots toward the tail. (**182**)

European Dragonet To 12 in. You won't find this fish along our coasts because it is a European species, but it is sometimes seen in aquariums. The male is very different from the female — golden brown with brilliant turquoise markings and a dorsal fin that is higher at the front. Pairs of these fish engage in an elaborate and beautiful courtship. (**183**)

Lancer Dragonet To 6½ in. This little American dragonet is a mottled red fish with a tall yellow dorsal fin. It lives in shallows off southern Florida in eelgrass beds. (**184**)

Neon Goby To 2 in. This little Atlantic goby is one of the "cleaner" fishes. It picks parasites off other fishes, which eagerly await its attentions. This goby has a black back and a glowing blue stripe along its side. As in many other gobies, the pelvic fins are modified to form a suction disc, which the fish uses to hold onto rocks or coral. (**185**)

Bluebanded Goby To 2½ in. This lovely little goby lives from central California southward and makes a good marine aquarium pet. It is bright orange with blue bands. (**186**)

Mudskipper To 11 in. This froggy-looking goby is a popular aquarium fish. In the Indo-Pacific it is found climbing out of brackish waters onto mud and roots in mangrove swamps. It is brown with black mottles that are usually sprinkled with little blue spots. (**187**)

Blue Tang To 14 in. This tang is also called a surgeonfish because it has a knife-like blade in a groove on each side of its tail. Surgeonfishes use this weapon to threaten or stab its enemies. Color this fish blue to purple-gray, with narrow stripes on the fins. Found in tropical Atlantic waters, it strays north to New York and west into the Gulf of Mexico. **(188)**

Naso Tang To 6 in. This Indo-European surgeonfish has two blades on each side of its tail. It has an elegant shape and is olive-gray with a black and yellow face and fins and a narrow blue iridescent line on its back. It is an attractive marine aquarium fish. **(189)**

Atlantic Mackerel To 22 in. Swift, schooling mackerels are found in all oceans. This one lives from Newfoundland to Cape Hatteras. It is dark blue or green above, with a silvery belly and wavy black lines on its back. Mackerels are important as food for people and other animals. **(190)**

Bluefin Tuna To 10 ft. This giant mackerel has weighed in at 1490 pounds. A commercially valuable fish, it is found in both our oceans from Labrador and Alaska south. It is blue-black above, grading to white below. The front part of its dorsal fin is sometimes yellowish; the second part is reddish. **(191)**

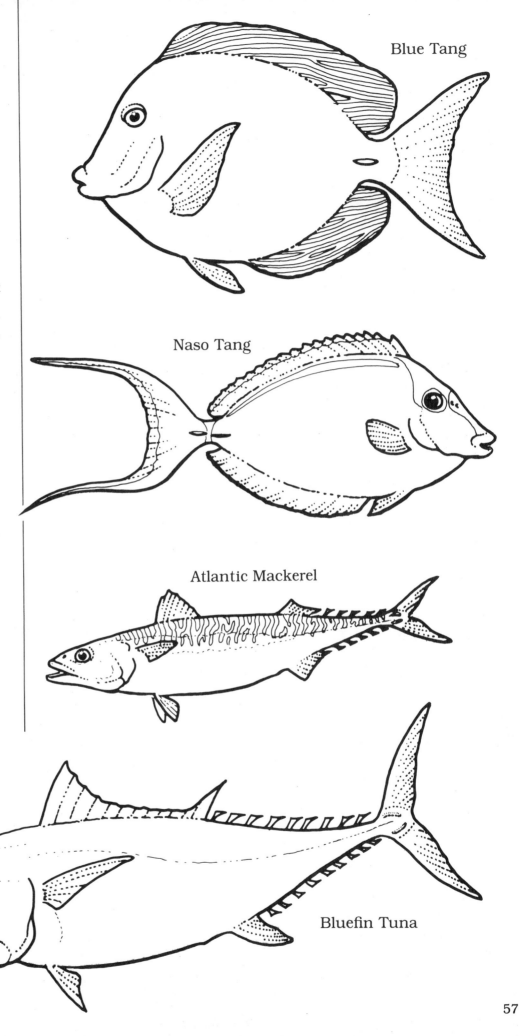

Blue Tang

Naso Tang

Atlantic Mackerel

Bluefin Tuna

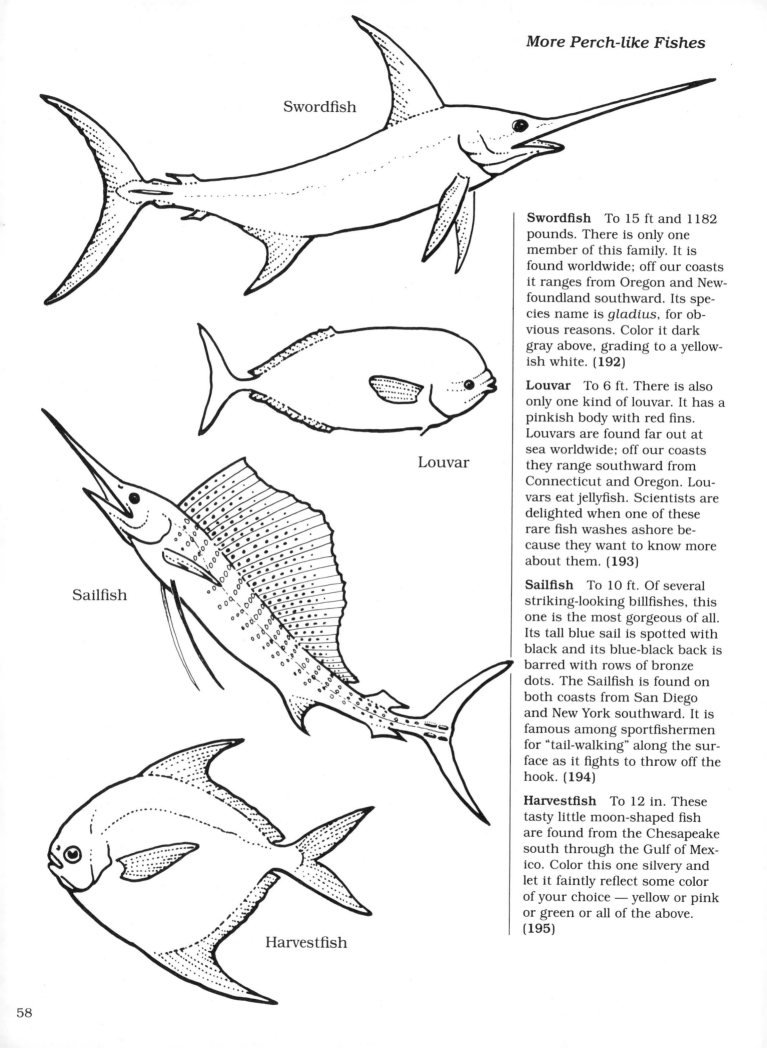

Swordfish

Louvar

Sailfish

Harvestfish

Swordfish To 15 ft and 1182 pounds. There is only one member of this family. It is found worldwide; off our coasts it ranges from Oregon and Newfoundland southward. Its species name is *gladius*, for obvious reasons. Color it dark gray above, grading to a yellowish white. (**192**)

Louvar To 6 ft. There is also only one kind of louvar. It has a pinkish body with red fins. Louvars are found far out at sea worldwide; off our coasts they range southward from Connecticut and Oregon. Louvars eat jellyfish. Scientists are delighted when one of these rare fish washes ashore because they want to know more about them. (**193**)

Sailfish To 10 ft. Of several striking-looking billfishes, this one is the most gorgeous of all. Its tall blue sail is spotted with black and its blue-black back is barred with rows of bronze dots. The Sailfish is found on both coasts from San Diego and New York southward. It is famous among sportfishermen for "tail-walking" along the surface as it fights to throw off the hook. (**194**)

Harvestfish To 12 in. These tasty little moon-shaped fish are found from the Chesapeake south through the Gulf of Mexico. Color this one silvery and let it faintly reflect some color of your choice — yellow or pink or green or all of the above. (**195**)

Climbing Perch To 10 in. This labyrinth fish lives in ditches and canals in Southeast Asia. In addition to normal gills, labyrinth fishes have an extra oxygen-absorbing organ that helps them survive in oxygen-poor water — or even on land. This organ enables the Climbing Perch to wriggle overland at night to find a new home when its puddle dries up. It is plain brown. **(196)**

Siamese Fighting Fish To 2 in. Bred for centuries in captivity, this aggressive fish is far more colorful than it was originally in nature in Southeast Asia. It too is a labyrinth fish. Color your male fish blue, yellow, or green. Female Siamese Fighting Fish are dull colored with shorter fins. **(197)**

Pearl Gourami To 4½ in. Another Asian labyrinth fish. The old males of this species are very beautiful, but they are a challenge to color. The easiest way to go about it is to start by lightly putting down a pale violet color *all over* the spotted areas — in between the spots too. Go over this with white colored pencil to blend it. *Then* go back and work over this pale background with a warm brown, leaving the spots light. Add a red throat and chest, and a black stripe from nose to tail. **(198)**

Paradise Fish To 3½ in. Here is another gorgeous labyrinth fish, also from Asia. It comes in a wide variety of colors. Why not give this male Paradise Fish a red body with blue stripes and a red tail with white stripes. **(199)**

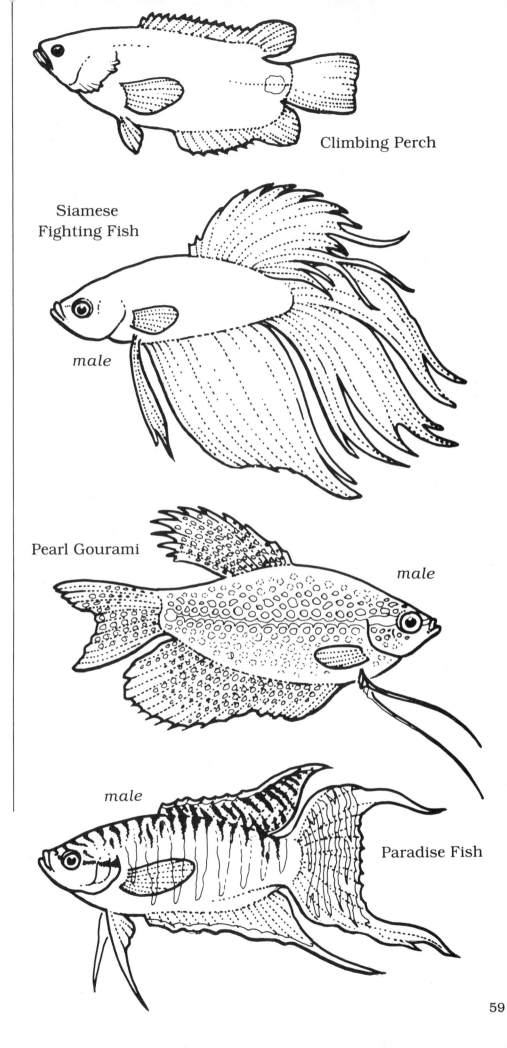

Climbing Perch

Siamese Fighting Fish

male

Pearl Gourami

male

male

Paradise Fish

59

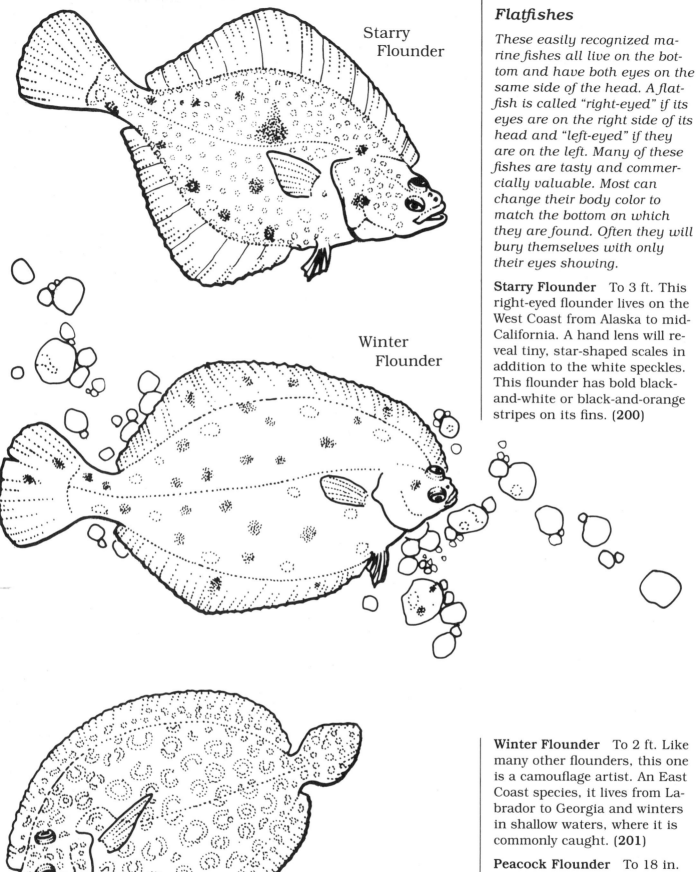

Starry
Flounder

Winter
Flounder

Peacock Flounder

Flatfishes

These easily recognized marine fishes all live on the bottom and have both eyes on the same side of the head. A flatfish is called "right-eyed" if its eyes are on the right side of its head and "left-eyed" if they are on the left. Many of these fishes are tasty and commercially valuable. Most can change their body color to match the bottom on which they are found. Often they will bury themselves with only their eyes showing.

Starry Flounder   To 3 ft. This right-eyed flounder lives on the West Coast from Alaska to mid-California. A hand lens will reveal tiny, star-shaped scales in addition to the white speckles. This flounder has bold black-and-white or black-and-orange stripes on its fins. **(200)**

Winter Flounder   To 2 ft. Like many other flounders, this one is a camouflage artist. An East Coast species, it lives from Labrador to Georgia and winters in shallow waters, where it is commonly caught. **(201)**

Peacock Flounder   To 18 in. This East Coast tropical flounder has very widely spaced eyes. It has pretty, dark-outlined blue crescents, circles, and spots all over its golden brown body. **(202)**

Naked Sole To 6 in. This scaleless little black-striped sole hides its pectoral fin beneath a flap of skin. It has small, close-set eyes. It lives over sand on the East Coast from Massachusetts to Florida. **(203)**

Hogchoker To 6 in. This small, black-lined sole has no pectoral fins at all. It occasionally ventures into fresh water along the coast of southeastern states. Does it choke hogs? No one knows. **(204)**

Atlantic Halibut To 8 ft. This huge East Coast flatfish can weigh up to 700 pounds and is usually caught by longlining far out at sea, over the banks where it lives. It is olive to gray with black mottling and has a large, fierce-looking mouth. The Pacific Halibut can be even larger than the Atlantic species — up to 800 pounds — and is a very valuable commercial fish. **(205)**

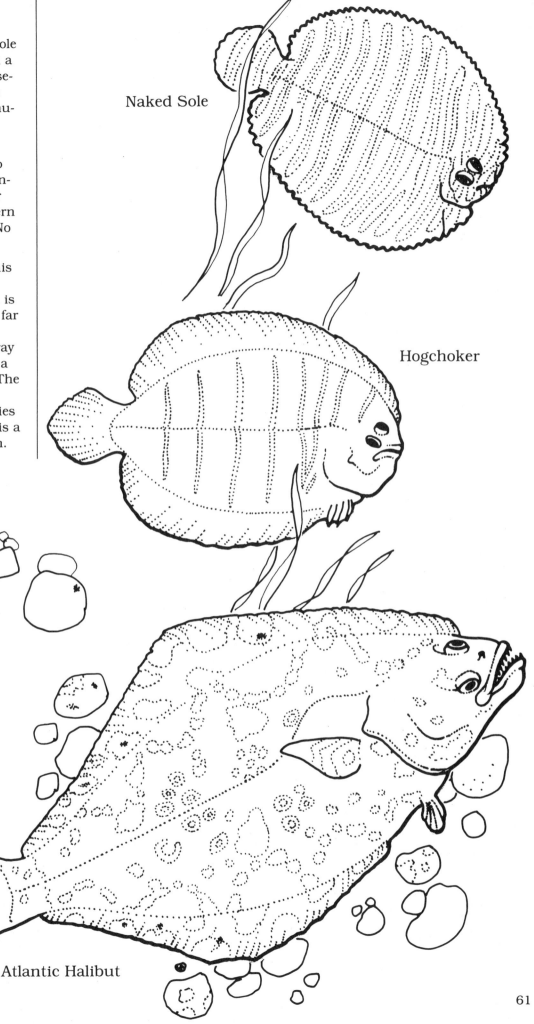

Naked Sole

Hogchoker

Atlantic Halibut

Queen Triggerfish

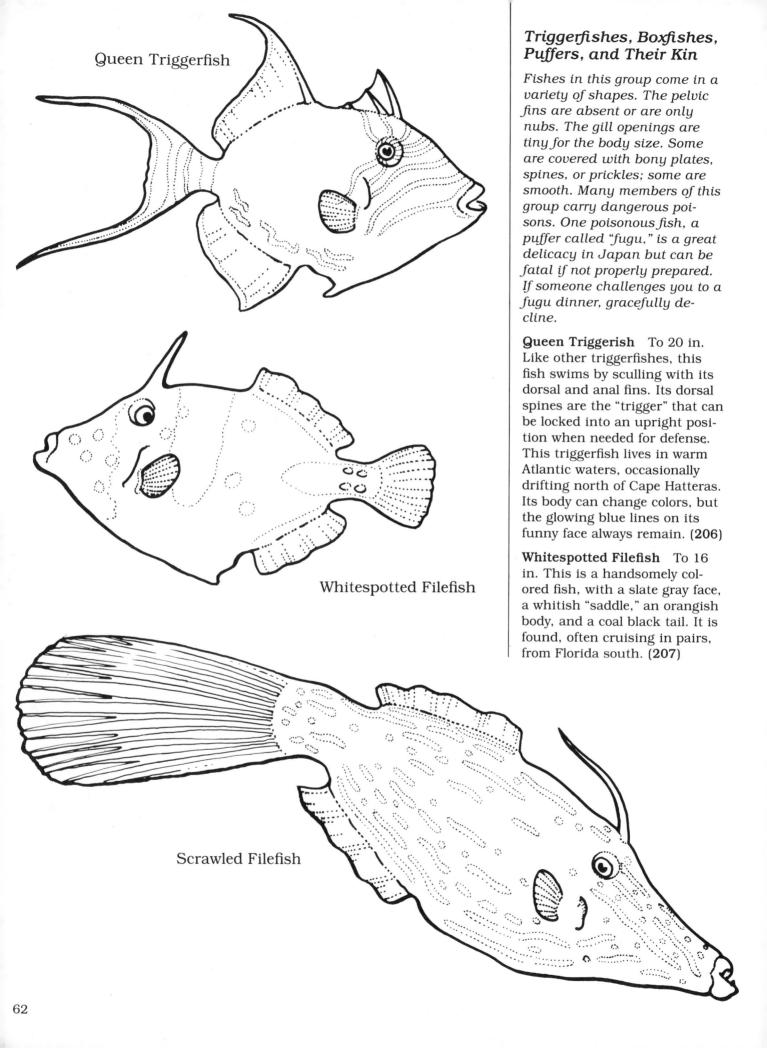

Whitespotted Filefish

Scrawled Filefish

Triggerfishes, Boxfishes, Puffers, and Their Kin

Fishes in this group come in a variety of shapes. The pelvic fins are absent or are only nubs. The gill openings are tiny for the body size. Some are covered with bony plates, spines, or prickles; some are smooth. Many members of this group carry dangerous poisons. One poisonous fish, a puffer called "fugu," is a great delicacy in Japan but can be fatal if not properly prepared. If someone challenges you to a fugu dinner, gracefully decline.

Queen Triggerish   To 20 in. Like other triggerfishes, this fish swims by sculling with its dorsal and anal fins. Its dorsal spines are the "trigger" that can be locked into an upright position when needed for defense. This triggerfish lives in warm Atlantic waters, occasionally drifting north of Cape Hatteras. Its body can change colors, but the glowing blue lines on its funny face always remain. **(206)**

Whitespotted Filefish   To 16 in. This is a handsomely colored fish, with a slate gray face, a whitish "saddle," an orangish body, and a coal black tail. It is found, often cruising in pairs, from Florida south. **(207)**

Scrawled Cowfish

Scrawled Filefish To 3 ft. This unmistakable fish has a flat body, a long snout, an overshot lower jaw, and a splendid large tail. Found worldwide in tropical waters, it is olive-gray with glowing blue lines and small black spots. It is a strange sight, swaying in the current with its head down slightly. **(208)**

Scrawled Cowfish To 18 in. As this appealing boxfish swims along in its bony covering, it looks like a little mechanical toy. Its blue-marked yellowish body is triangular in cross-section. This fish is found in warm Atlantic waters, occasionally drifting north to Massachusetts. **(209)**

Bandtail Puffer

Bandtail Puffer To 12 in. This little spotted puffer can be found from Massachusetts southward, over turtle grass beds and reef rubble. Like other puffers, it can inflate its body with water or air. This fish is highly toxic — don't eat one. **(210)**

Ocean Sunfish

Ocean Sunfish To 10 ft. This oceanic giant is one of the largest bony fishes. It is found all over the world. Improbable as it looks, it is a strong swimmer. It eats jellyfish. **(211)**

Porcupinefish

Porcupinefish To 3 ft. This spiny and spotted puffer is found worldwide in warm seas. It uses the two strong teeth in the front of its mouth to crush the hard shells of animals that most other fish cannot eat. **(212)**

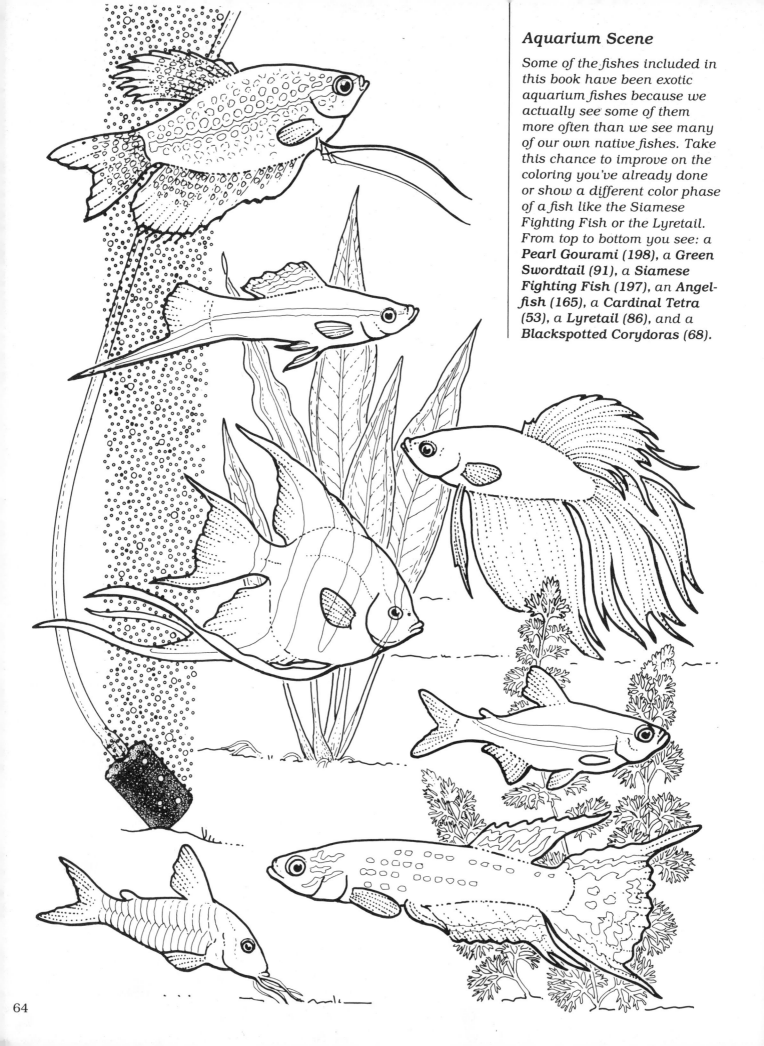

Aquarium Scene

Some of the fishes included in this book have been exotic aquarium fishes because we actually see some of them more often than we see many of our own native fishes. Take this chance to improve on the coloring you've already done or show a different color phase of a fish like the Siamese Fighting Fish or the Lyretail. From top to bottom you see: a **Pearl Gourami (198)**, a **Green Swordtail (91)**, a **Siamese Fighting Fish (197)**, an **Angelfish (165)**, a **Cardinal Tetra (53)**, a **Lyretail (86)**, and a **Blackspotted Corydoras (68)**.

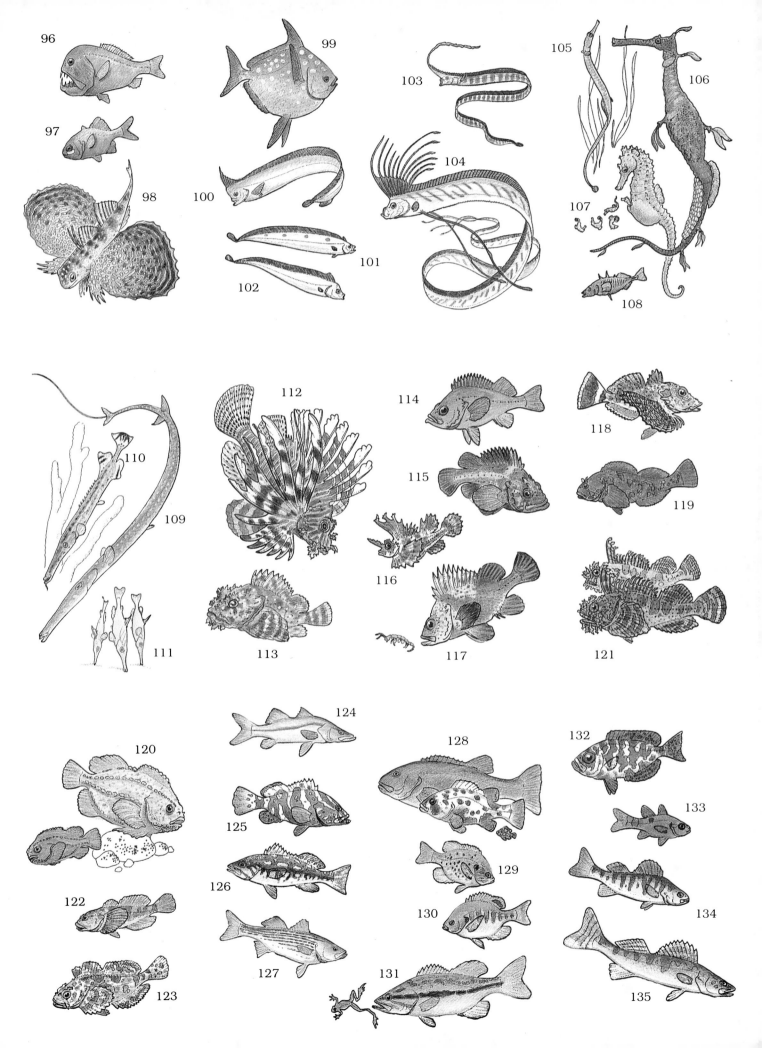

96

97

98

99

100

101

102

103

104

105

106

107

108

109

110

111

112

113

114

115

116

117

118

119

120

121

122

123

124

125

126

127

128

129

130

131

132

133

134

135

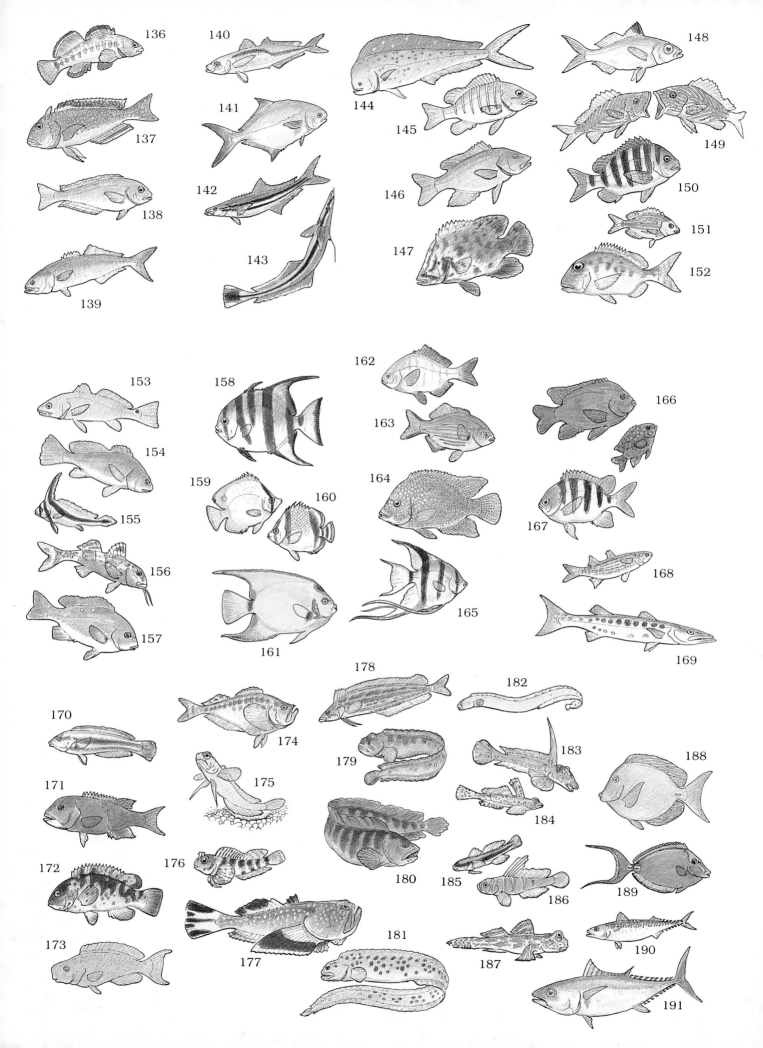